Ageless Beauty

Ageless Beauty

The secrets to French elegance

Clémence von Mueffling

with Karen Moline

MICHAEL JOSEPH
an imprint of
PENGUIN BOOKS

MICHAEL JOSEPH

UK | USA | Canada | Ireland | Australia
India | New Zealand | South Africa

Michael Joseph is part of the Penguin Random House group of companies
whose addresses can be found at global.penguinrandomhouse.com

Penguin
Random House
UK

This book is not intended to provide medical advice. You should
consult a medical professional in matters relating to health,
especially if you have existing medical conditions. Readers,
especially those with existing health problems, should consult their
physician or health care professional before adopting certain dietary
or fitness choices. The fact that an organization or website is
mentioned in the book as a potential source of information does
not mean that the author or publisher endorse any of the
information they may provide or recommendations they may make.

First published in the United States as *Ageless Beauty the French Way* by St Martin's Press 2018
Published in Great Britain as *Ageless Beauty* by Michael Joseph 2018
001

Printed in Great Britain by Clays Ltd, St Ives plc

A CIP catalogue record for this book is available from the British Library

HARDBACK ISBN: 978-0-718-18854-2
OM PAPERBACK ISBN: 978-0-241-35845-0

www.greenpenguin.co.uk

MIX
Paper from
responsible sources
FSC® C018179

Penguin Random House is committed to a
sustainable future for our business, our readers
and our planet. This book is made from Forest
Stewardship Council® certified paper.

To William, Anaïs, and Lucas,

les ADMV

Contents

Part Four

Les Cheveux

Part Five

Life et les Bonnes Habitudes

Introduction

Beauty is pure magic that transforms the nature of existence.

—JEAN D'ORMESSON, *GUIDE DES ÉGARÉS*

I like to joke that I was born in a jar.

My mother and grandmother were both beauty editors at French *Vogue*. They taught me, in their inimitable French way, that beauty is an attitude, a way of taking care of yourself. Not only were they strong female role models, but they also devoted their lives to discovering the most outstanding and effective products and treatments for women of all ages, then shared this information with their readers.

I would always count the days until Christmas, when my mother would receive boxes of one gorgeous item after another, sent by the most prestigious brands trying to outdo each other in creativity, attempting to seduce the beauty journalists. L'Oréal will forever stay in my memory as the creators of the *boîte magique*—the magic box. Their Christmas gift was always cylindrical, like an enormous hatbox, overflowing with all their latest fragrances, creams, and makeup products. My sister and I were always beside ourselves with joy, lifting that magical lid and fighting over who got to try the different products first.

My idea of heaven was being allowed to go with my mother to her office at *Vogue*, sitting on her little sofa and looking at the shelves of beauty products, trying on a new lipstick, and observing the other editors, busy and intense, with a noticeable confidence and *savoir-faire* in their style.

My mother and grandmother taught me that skincare starts young. I still remember the day my mother showed me how to clean my face impeccably before going to bed (at a mere thirteen years old).

That summer, I was sent to summer camp in the United States to improve my English. Inside my brand-new suitcase, my mother had carefully packed a bottle of Estée perfume by Estée Lauder, a Lierac stretch mark cream, and a Clarins Eau Dynamisante moisturizing body lotion infamous for its pungent aroma. I still remember the shocked looks I got from my bunkmates when I rubbed some of the Lierac cream on my thighs. Their shock quickly turned to horror as they witnessed me applying some Clarins moisturizer onto my legs after I showered. Though these girls were my age, they had not yet begun any kind of beauty ritual. They thought I was crazy—but they were also happy to learn my techniques!

My mother, Lorraine Bolloré, began her career as an assistant on photo shoots during the haute couture collections at American *Vogue* in 1969. She was trained, as her mother had been, under the stern eye of Susan Train, who was still the Paris-based correspondent for American *Vogue*, then edited by Diana Vreeland. After two years working for the makeup line Eve of Roma, in 1969 she returned to French *Vogue*, this time as an assistant beauty editor when the dynamic Robert Caillé was the editor-in-chief. In 1979 she became beauty editor-in-chief of French *Vogue*. She left in the early 1990s at the peak of her career after twice winning the famous Prix Jasmin, given each year to the best beauty journalist in the fragrance category working in France.

My grandmother Régine Debrise not only expected her daughter to look impeccable but her granddaughters as well. She would tell my sister and me, *"Rendez-vous* for dinner with some Rimmel mascara," and we knew that, at minimum, she expected us to wear makeup, even for a casual Sunday dinner. The thought of us at the table sans mascara was inconceivable—*impossible*!

Régine began her career as a model in 1947, when she was seventeen. Her first photo shoot was with Arik Nepo, for French *Vogue*. Three years later, she began posing for acclaimed photographer Irving Penn, appearing on the cover of *Vogue* in October 1950—Penn's first French *Vogue* cover! She also worked with Henry Clarke for another *Vogue* cover published in July 1951. In 1957, she began her career with American *Vogue* under the tutelage of Susan Train during the Grande Exposition Internationale in Barcelona. She then joined the French *Vogue* team in Paris and remained there for several years. In those days, the women who worked at French *Vogue* were, in addition to their jobs as editors, also ambassadors for the magazine; you could recognize a *femme de Vogue* through a specific style that the editor-in-chief at the time called "Vogueish." It involved elegance in both their attitude and mannerisms, and a look that always included flawless stockings, high heels, and a feminine fragrance.

Because skincare and the beauty business were such an important part of my mother's and grandmother's lives, I decided to become the third generation of woman in my family to work in the beauty industry. When I moved to New York City, I started to understand that French women grasped the connection between beauty and wellness in a way that I wasn't seeing in America, and I wanted to bridge that gap. This realization inspired me to create an online magazine in 2014, *Beauty and Well Being* (*BWB*), as I was committed to helping women everywhere live a healthy, balanced lifestyle. I knew that skincare wasn't just about using a really expensive cream on your face. If you are not sleeping well, you are never going to look your best; if you are not eating a healthy diet, your skin will never glow; if you're not enjoying life and savoring every moment—what the French call *joie de vivre*—it will show on your face. Beauty and wellness are about accepting who you are, making the most of what you have, and, as I always remind the readers of my magazine, being happy with the small changes you make to improve your daily routine, because real change is hard.

When *BWB* was launched, I brought together a global team of twenty writers, all experts in their field and united by their passion for beauty, health, and wellness. We cover everything from makeup trends and products that make a difference to tips on nutrition and exercise, recipes, in-depth features, and profiles on experts in their specialties. Most of all, *BWB* values long-term, holistic solutions based on solid research and proven results.

In a youth-obsessed society, *BWB* is a proud pioneer in the publishing world, addressing women from their twenties to their sixties—and beyond. We believe there is no age limit to beauty, balance, and happiness. With this book, I have expanded the mission of *BWB* to share what three generations of French beauty experts have lived and learned.

I was very lucky to have access to insider advice from across the generations and to be exposed to the best French tips and tricks that help a woman look her best at all stages of her life. In this book, I will be giving you a glimpse of what you can look forward to generations from now. I am so lucky that I can look at my mother and grandmother and know exactly what awaits me, and I am so grateful they are still here to guide me.

Add to this my training as a journalist, which has transformed me into an antenna that captures all the highly sought-after information from world-class experts. In this book, I'll share the newest and most useful information about skin- and hair-care products and treatments. I'll also show you how French women are able to apply that information and combine it with smart lifestyle choices (and the occasional cheat!) to always look their best. You'll soon see that the French attitude toward beauty is to make very small changes over the years, and to work hard at prevention and maintenance to stave off problems before they occur. Taking care of yourself and availing yourself of the countless options for skincare will give you visible results—for now, and for the rest of your life.

"We are, after all, going to see generations who are going to stay younger. Overall, we are going to live longer and better," says Odile Mohen, Consumer and Market Insight Global Director for L'Oréal Research and Innovation.

Ageless Beauty the French Way will also teach you the French lesson that you're never too old to change how you take care of your skin and health. My grandmother is a testament to this. Last summer, she had a little knee pain and was given pain patches to wear at night. After a few days, she realized that the skin around her knee was softer, with fewer wrinkles, and so she decided to try the patches on her face. She cut one and carefully applied the pieces to her cheeks and forehead. When she returned to the pharmacy, she proudly told the pharmacist what she was doing. The pharmacist's jaw dropped. She proceeded to very gently suggest that, perhaps, due to the potency of the ingredients in the patch, my grandmother was better off keeping them on her knee. She was crushed! But you have to admire her gumption. She's always ready to try something new, a habit that not only keeps her looking amazingly beautiful but fosters a remarkably youthful attitude as well. This is why *Ageless Beauty the French Way* was created for women of *all* ages!

THREE GENERATIONS OF BEAUTY ADVICE

In this book you will find the *crème de la crème* of French experts, whose clientele includes French actresses, models, and high-society women. You'll meet facialists, dermatologists, and plastic surgeons, makeup artists, hairstylists, and manicurists—from those who use traditional methods to those on the cutting edge of technology. I have infused this book with the most up-to-date information and assembled a gold mine collection of beauty expertise. I know you will find their advice both practical and fascinatingly French.

Part 1, "French Beauty Rituals from Three Generations," is an overview of how my grandmother, mother, and I were raised with inimitable French ideas about beauty. Part 2, "Le Visage" (French for *Face*), will teach you the most beneficial way to take care of your skin, particularly cleansing, with the most useful anti-aging tips you can do yourself—no doctor intervention necessary. Inspired by my mother and grandmother, I have organized the content in this part of the book to target three different age groups: *jeunesse* (youth) for twenty- to thirty-five-year-olds, *plén-*

itude (abundance) for ages thirty-five to fifty-five, and *maturité* (maturity) for women fifty-five and over. Your skincare needs in your twenties are going to shift a few years later, and you should change what you use and how you use it accordingly. Women are smart enough consumers to know how much Photoshop is being used in ads for beauty products, but they are still confused by the sheer variety of products to choose from. My mother and grandmother provide their input based on their decades of experience interspersed with their very personal memories of the fascinating people they met and worked with, as well as their knowledge of the most helpful skincare products and treatments for women as they grow older.

Throughout the book, I recommend specific products and brands in general that reflect the personal, mostly French-based choices of my family as well as the experts I interviewed. As beauty editors, we have tested and sampled thousands of products over the years and have included many that I would call *grands classiques* in this book, as we know they work and have never failed us. We're only sorry that we couldn't list more of the incredible products available, as there are so many fantastic items for you to try—but we needed to be judicious. With so many choices, I know you'll find the perfect product for all your needs.

The same format is followed in part 3, "Le Corps" (*Body*), with three generations of beauty editors sharing their knowledge. In part 4, "Les Cheveux" (*Hair*), you'll learn how to take care of your tresses, and several of the most celebrated French hair experts in the world will share their advice about their latest discoveries and treatments so you can have the best hair possible.

Finally, in part 5, "Life et les Bonnes Habitudes" (*Life and Good Habits*), my experts and I will share our favorite tips for changing how you eat, move, exercise, and sleep—all of which will, of course, improve the health and appearance of your skin. Last but not least, I'll talk about the very French love of perfume.

I hope you will enjoy reading this book as much as I enjoyed interviewing so many of France's most renowned beauty specialists. I am thrilled to share their advice with you. I also want you to use this book as a beauty bible for the ages—for the timeless advice that will be as useful to you at twenty-five as it will be when you're seventy. If you have a good foundation for your skincare, what you're doing now will serve you in good stead throughout your entire life. I marvel at the beauty of my mother's and grandmother's skin, and I know they still have the glow because their beauty regimen was very important to them. They avoided the sun, they used the best possible products they could afford, they massaged their faces, and they happily visited their local *instituts de beauté* as often as they could.

As my grandmother is so fond of saying, "You are never too old to learn—and to look even better!" Just as she once did for me, I have a little secret drawer at home where I keep some of my favorite beauty products for my daughter. I load it up with sample bottles of perfume, cute lip balms, or new brushes. It is like a delightful place full of hidden treasures for her. We already share fun moments when I put my makeup on, and she happily grabs one of my brushes to copy me.

Bonne lecture!

Part One

French Beauty Rituals from Three Generations

Chapter 1

The Art of French Beauty at Any Age

Beauty begins the moment you decide to be yourself.

—COCO CHANEL

I grew up in Paris with my sister and brother in a very traditional way. Our parents worked, and we were very fortunate that both sets of grandparents had a lot of influence on how we were raised. My maternal grandmother, Régine, often picked us up from school, and I have so many wonderful memories of seeing her waiting for me. She would wear elegant cashmere turtlenecks, always with a lovely brooch pinned to the side, or a chic blouse in the summer months with matching-color clip earrings. She'd never dream of leaving the house without her red lipstick on, and I'd always end up with sweet lipstick marks on my cheeks. Her car was scented with a touch of her favorite fragrance that she spritzed on with abandon. After school, we'd drive to her house, often stopping by one of the sophisticated bakeries like the famous Carette for a brioche or—her favorite—a chocolate éclair. And on the happiest of happy days, I'd be invited to my mother's office at French *Vogue*, which, for a little girl enthralled by beauty products and perfumes, was like being taken on a magic carpet ride to a cave of wonders.

There were the days when my sister and I would sit and watch our mother get ready to go out for the night. We'd watch her apply her makeup with a sure hand, enormous rollers perched on her head so she could give herself an expert 'do, something I've never quite been able to do myself! Then, after she was dressed, she'd gaze at her collection of perfumes before deciding on the one that best suited her mood. What a great lesson that was—to trust your instincts about what felt good in the moment and to always be willing to experiment. She always smelled so delicious.

Once I hit those teenage years and my skin needed help, my mother would take me to our local *pharmacie,* where I would get the gentle lecture about acne and proper cleansing. I would also save all my pocket money to order the famous Embellisseur Abricot by Agnès b., a complexion enhancer that was sold back then via a catalog called *Club des Créateurs de Beauté* (the Beauty Creators' Club), which featured a line aimed at teenagers with blemish-prone skin among its large selection of makeup and skincare. My friends and I hoped it would make us look like Laetitia Casta, who was on the cusp of becoming a famous French model at the time. Then, when The Body Shop opened in Paris, we were thrilled, because the products were affordable, and everything smelled so good. The store was very different, and you felt cool just sitting in there. For us French girls, it was so *English*!

I also have fond memories of the magazine *Jeune et Jolie*, which translates to *Young and Pretty*. It was, for French teenagers, a combination of *Seventeen* and *Cosmopolitan*. I used money from my allowance to get a subscription when I was fifteen, and I was so proud of myself when I wrote out a check from my first bank account. As soon as the issue arrived every month, I'd practically devour it, especially the beauty section, until one day my dad got the mail before I did, and there was the newest issue, with a headline blaring on the cover about what to do when your boyfriend can't perform in bed. My sweet and overprotective father was so shocked that he banned the magazine, even though I begged and pleaded for him to change his mind. From that moment onward, I'd still read it every month at my friends' houses instead!

What beauty lessons did I learn growing up in France?

AT THE CORE OF FRENCH BEAUTY BELIEFS

Parisian women . . . want above all to become the best possible version of themselves, outside and in, at any age.
—ANNE BEREST, AUDREY DIWAN,
CAROLINE DE MAIGRET, AND SOPHIE MAS,
HOW TO BE PARISIAN WHEREVER YOU ARE

Beauty Is Not About "Perfection"

French women like to give the impression of a combination of dedication and *laisser aller* (which means letting themselves go) when it comes to beauty. Yes, we love our polished beauty that appears so effortless but that we know takes time and dedication. We can spend hours finding the ideal shade of lipstick, the color that will sublimely enhance our lips, while our hair might have only warranted a few cursory strokes of the brush as we dashed out the door. Definitely not perfect! As my sister once explained to me, she understands the things that men look at when they see a woman, and that what is not perfect can sometimes be charming, and what is already perfect does not need to be overdone.

French women like the idea of healthy skin, but it does not have to be flawless. What I have noticed with my friends in Paris and those in New York is that the Parisiennes have a healthy beauty routine but will not give up everything to obtain perfect results. In fact, for many of them, if perfect skin is at the cost of not eating any more cheese or a croissant for breakfast, or taking a nap on a sunny beach, they will settle for skin that is just good enough! Going to any extreme in a vain search for "perfection" will never leave anyone satisfied.

According to Isabelle Bellis, a French-born, New York–based holistic facialist, "The basics are an essential starting point. My French clients believe in a simple skincare regimen, are very disciplined, and love manual face massage. In general, they are less aggressive with their skin. Regardless of age, they are always coquettish, and not as concerned with aging as much as aging *gracefully*. The reality and existence of wrinkles are not as important as the quality and health of their skin, which needs to be perfectly plump and soft. Well-hydrated skin that is dewy and glowing optimally reflects light in a flattering way that makes it look almost like silk. So skin quality is paramount, as we prefer bare skin and minimal makeup—think classic red lipstick and mascara."

Add a smile, *et voilà*!

We Love Our Beauty Brands and Our Local Shops Where We Can Buy Them

One of the reasons French women seem knowledgeable about skin is that we get such good advice from our neighborhood *pharmacies.* These are like our cafés, restaurants, and corner bakeries—they're fixtures found in every *quartier* in every small town and every big city. For many years, French women did not go to the spa for beauty products, and French doctors did not have their own skincare lines, so the pharmacists were highly trained to recommend specific products from a wide range of different brands and for different budgets.

We also are addicted to our neighborhood *institut de beauté.* No matter how small the town, there is a salon for our beauty treatments (waxing, manicures, facials, massage, eyelash tints, etc.). They are usually small and rather simple salons, but we start going to them as teenagers, so we grow up with the aestheticians and they become like family. Or, if we have time for a treat, we'll go to one of the larger salons or spas. For my mother and grandmother, there were the fabled Payot, Ingrid Millet, Orlane, Françoise Morice, or the American salons Elizabeth Arden and Helena Rubinstein (who were always in competition with each other!).

And of course we love our local cafés where the waiters call us *mademoiselle* with a big smile—instead of *madame,* which makes you feel so old!

Beauty Products and Treatments Aren't Just About Making Us Look Better but About *Feeling* Better, Too—They're Always Going to Be a Regular Part of Our Lives

One gloomy day in Paris, I woke up and looked out the window and realized that fall was truly gone, and it was one of those gray winter-is-coming days with low-hanging clouds turning everything all monochrome and dreary, with a chilly drizzle to compound the misery. There was only one thing to do: go to my neighborhood *parfumerie* and buy Clarins Masvelt (body shaping cream). It had a unique buttery texture and divine scent, and I remember how it made me feel so much better just by applying some to my hands and taking these few minutes of pampering.

To this day I still have my selection of "feel-good products" that I will use to give me that extra boost on days when I need it the most. I think this is one of the reasons why the French are so dedicated to their beauty regimens, and we make sure to have a budget for them just as we have a budget for taking care of our teeth or for going to a gym or pool.

It's a part of our lives—one that we know will make us feel better.

Making beauty a part of your life doesn't have to be costly or time-consuming. For example, when I talk about double cleansing in the next chapter, while you might have to buy two different cleansers at first, in the long run you'll be using less of each. Ditto with my moisturizers; I have several with SPF for the daytime and richer ones for use when my skin needs extra hydration or in the wintertime. They last for a long time because I rotate them depending on the weather and how my skin feels. And when you use good products with a high concentration of top-quality and effective ingredients, you use less of them.

For me, it's the little *je ne sais quoi* that makes beauty self-care so rewarding: The trace of perfume in the wake of someone else walking by, or discovering the perfect shade of red or pink lipstick that makes your whole face come alive. A particular pleasure is having a local salon that makes you feel welcome the instant you walk in the door, where you're a regular and have a warm and engaging personal relationship with the aestheticians who will always do their utmost to make you look and feel your best, even if you only made an appointment to get your eyebrows waxed.

Little things add up to a much fuller beauty experience!

Subtle Is the Secret Ingredient of French Beauty

My mother and grandmother often told me something that Yves Saint Laurent was known to say: "We must never confuse elegance with snobbery." They meant that we have to find what suits us. For example, my grandmother never uses eyeliner, as she knows it makes her eyes look too droopy. A famous photographer once told my mother to enhance either her eyes or her lips but never both, and she has followed this advice ever since. Yes, sometimes you need less than you think *et tant mieux*!

I saw proof of their advice when I was growing up. A woman *d'un certain âge* from a South American country was the most elegant woman in our neighborhood. Even though she was in her seventies, I never saw her without an impeccable chignon (a sophisticated version of a bun), a light dusting of powder, a hint of mascara, and a cool red lipstick on her lips. She had an impossibly long neck and loved to wear a brocade coat that swirled slightly as she walked gracefully, with precise posture. I thought she was as regal as the queens we learned about in history class. Her simple elegance gave a great message to younger generations.

Another equally elegant woman I met several times when I was working for the Spanish family-owned business Puig in Barcelona was the designer Carolina Herrera. I was in my very early twenties at the time, and she left an indelible impression. She basically was in uniform: a crisp white tailored shirt with the collar turned up just a little bit to frame and enhance her face, and slim black trousers. Her jewelry was simple yet very chic, perhaps a few gold bangle bracelets. She knew what suited her, and *she* wore *it,* rather that *it* wearing *her*—which is what many of my friends and I had not yet learned at the time. (Well, we were young, after all!)

My sister is another wonderful example of knowing what suits her. She has beautiful long hair that falls around her shoulders like a necklace, and her gorgeous eyebrows perfectly frame her face. For her it is all about never going overboard with makeup, colors, or accessories. It is a look that she has made her own.

Perfume Is a French Woman's Signature

We French women love our *parfumeries,* the small shops dedicated to a large assortment of perfumes. These stores have a marvelous selection of well-chosen products along with knowledgeable *vendeuses,* the saleswomen who help you decide what to buy. They'll always fill your bag at the end with samples and offer to spray you with perfume before you leave.

I'll discuss this in much more detail in Chapter 10, but know for now that a French woman doesn't consider herself dressed unless she's wearing perfume, even if it can put her in a delicate situation. My sister recently reminded me that when she was a teenager, in the process of sneaking out from the house at night to meet some friends, I once caught her because I could smell the delicious waft of her perfume even though I was in my bedroom and she was tiptoeing down the hallway. I got out of bed, realized she had just left, and wrote, "I know you went out. Your perfume gave you away!" on a Post-it and stuck it on her door. She loved it so much that she kept the note!

My mother adored her perfume collection, as you know. And

my father was a scent devotee as well. One of my earliest memories of him is how clean and well-groomed his hands were and how wonderfully they smelled from the Roger&Gallet soaps he used. To me, he was and still is the epitome of subtle, masculine Parisian chic.

As for me, I still think back fondly to the few months I spent working at the Clarins UK offices when I was finishing my studies. I had of course already tried and liked some of their products thanks to my mother, but while on the job I was introduced to so many new products that I fell in love with that brand, with their message, and the wonderful scents of their creams. The founder, Jacques Courtin-Clarins, launched his now-famous Eau Dynamisante with the line "the feel-good fragrance." And that is how I feel every time I spray some on.

Most of All, Stick to a Routine

One of the most important components of any French woman's beauty routine is just that—it's a routine. We know how important it is to have a schedule and to stick to it. To persevere even when you don't feel like it. Really, who wants to spend any time taking off mascara and giving her face a thorough cleaning after a long day at work? Not *moi*! But I have a cleansing routine, and I will never go to sleep without following it. It's so deeply ingrained now that I don't even think about it. I just do it, no matter what.

In other words, we love our polished appearance that might look so effortless, but it does take time and dedication.

My grandmother also tells me, quite often, that the older you get, the more disciplined you have to be. In fact, it was her own mother who taught her that—as she puts it, the bed is your worst enemy as you grow older because you get tired more easily and want to stay in your nice, warm, and comfy sheets. Grandmother Régine is eighty-seven and in that phase of her life. She's fighting it, but it's an everyday fight. She gets up and goes out, and she loves the step-counting app on her phone because she can get immediate, satisfying feedback on how far she walks.

And on those days when my grandmother would rather stay in bed, she thinks of her brother Guy d'Estribaud, and then she gets motivated! At ninety-six years old, Uncle Guy is still so good-looking. He's tall and fit, with a naughty twinkle in his eye. He has the face, neck, and hands of a much, much younger man, to the envy of his friends who are decades younger. When we travel together, in fact, and he hands his passport over to the authorities at the airport, they look at him in sheer astonishment—because he was born in 1922! He's still full of energy and is so witty that he always makes me laugh. I just adore him!

Uncle Guy lives in Biarritz and still does everything by himself. He gets up at 7:00 a.m. on the dot, makes himself a large, healthy breakfast, and then he goes to the market—without a shopping list, mind you, as he wants to make sure he keeps his brain sharp—to get fresh food for the rest of the day or two. He doesn't have a car, so he walks everywhere. His posture is always perfect, and I never dare slouch around him, as it's such an inspiration to see how beautifully straight he sits. He goes back home, cooks his lunch, takes a big nap, and cleans up around the house or maybe sees a friend. At 6:00 p.m. he watches the news, then he has what we'd consider a snack for dinner—perhaps a piece of cheese with some little whole-grain crackers, or a yogurt.

When my uncle is tired, he puts his head on the pillow and sleeps soundly through the night until seven in the morning. He never, ever wakes up in the middle of the night, and he never needs an alarm clock. I asked him what his trick was, and he said simply, "It's not complicated. I just get away from myself." He has no electronics. No cell phone. And boom, down he goes.

My uncle doesn't think of his routine as being boring; it's something that helps him thrive. It gives structure to his days. So if you look at your beauty regimen not as a challenge but as merely part of your daily routine, like brushing your teeth or taking a shower, it becomes so much easier to stick to it. You'll see how to do this in the next five chapters, where you'll learn how to take moments for yourself, moments of pleasure, and moments of beauty.

HOW FRENCH BEAUTY IDEAS HAVE SHIFTED OVER THE LAST FIFTY YEARS

The most significant change is that French beauty used to be about ultrasophistication and glamour—but often at the cost of comfort. Today, to be more comfortable, we choose clothing and shoes that are easier to wear and beauty habits that are easier to maintain. Beauty codes are more about a natural look and looks that suit working women who lead active lives. From our hairstyles to our makeup, the idea is that women should be able to look nice in the morning *and* in the evening for a cocktail in less time, too. It is a less sophisticated femininity.

Both my mother and grandmother enjoy all the benefits of new textures and formulas that make their makeup look less "done" and leave their skin fresher after they remove it at night. They are still their sophisticated selves—but now, with ease! And as you'll see, it wasn't always this way.

RÉGINE: American *Vogue* had rented a small apartment that our editor had found, to have Dior's and Balenciaga's haute couture collections for fall/winter 1950 photographed by Irving Penn. That studio, which had once been a painter's atelier, was on the top floor because Penn preferred to work with daylight, with a minimum of artificial lighting, and it had an enormous skylight. It was also unbearably hot on that particular August day, made even more difficult as we were wearing winter dresses and coats. We were so hot that our makeup started melting. I was used to that, because the heat of the lights in other studios made it melt, too, and fortunately all I had applied that day was just a touch of mascara, a little powder, and bright red lipstick. (I pulled my hair back because I knew I'd be wearing hats.)

I also wasn't too worried, as I was modeling that day with the lovely Lisa Fonssagrives, who was married to Penn. I loved working with her, as she was such a lovely person to be around. Lisa had studied ballet for years and had impeccable posture and ease with her body. She could hold poses for ages, although we didn't have time for a long and involved shoot, as the dresses had to be taken by bike messengers, who were usually the photographers' assistants, to buyers or other magazine editors the minute we were done with them. These cyclists would cross the Seine to pick up some last-minute accessories from the designers to enhance the shoot. Everything had to be perfect, of course—but, above all, it was crucial to shoot the collections before any other magazine. Penn would indicate what he wanted, and insist on a calm atmosphere for the shoot. I was very focused because the jacket I was wearing was too big, so we had to make it look smaller by putting some large clothespins in the back— and I could hardly breathe for fear of making the clothespins pop off. We'd only take breaks so Lisa and I could redo our melting makeup!

Having to do my own makeup was a great way to instill good skills. Even today I still like a very sophisticated look. At my age, I have switched to a lighter makeup, but I still use the following essentials every day: mascara, blush, and lipstick. I have learned to never look *négligée*—as in those days, women would never, ever look anything less than perfectly polished!

When I look back at that shoot, two things stand out. I have always loved that pose, which Clémence once told me reminded her of hieroglyphics of Egyptian princesses. The structured shape of the outfit, with its very nipped-in waist and enhanced shoulder line, is softened thanks to the luxurious large cashmere scarf around it that Penn placed on one side and then the other until he was satisfied. A little red velvet hat adorned with ostrich feather, whose lightness perfectly balanced the flow of the scarf, made the ensemble complete.

And this photograph also makes me realize how much beauty trends have changed. I grew up with very specific codes that were more sophisticated and glamorous, but women had to look very perfect or they would be judged accordingly. Today, it is perfectly acceptable to favor a more casual look.

What an amazing experience for my grandmother! As for the photo with the pearl necklace, also by Irving Penn, I rediscovered it a few years ago. When I was working for Dior in Paris, the company always held an end-of-the-year meeting for all the employees. We were invited to meet inside the Dior laboratory, which was located just outside of Paris, where all the creams and fragrances were concocted and created. It was a special day for everyone, and we would sit in a large auditorium while the different teams presented all the new products that were about to be released in the upcoming months. When the perfume team began their presentation, this marvelous photo of my grandmother appeared on a large screen, an image of her wearing an incredibly chic dress with a long pearl necklace looped around her neck and placed delicately over her left shoulder. I was unbelievably thrilled that they were using her as the epitome of Dior elegance, but I was way too shy to dare to say that the gorgeous woman in that photo was my beloved grandmother! (This photo can be seen in the color insert.)

Over fifty years later, my grandmother was coming to visit me in New York, and she wrote Penn a letter telling him she would be spending a few days in Manhattan. He immediately replied, asking her to come see him. They had a warm and emotional reunion in his photo studio on lower Fifth Avenue. Penn was so happy to see her, and he asked her to tell him as many stories as she could about Lisa, whom he adored and was missing terribly, as she had died a few years before. It was as if all the years melted away and they were once again working together in a boiling-hot garret in Paris, and laughing about my grandmother's melting makeup.

LORRAINE: During the time I worked for American *Vogue,* I was an assistant for photo shoots. I was lucky to be chosen to help during the haute couture collections in the late 1960s with Bert Stern—the photographer best known for the last photo shoot Marilyn Monroe ever did—helping with the fittings. I was a bit tempted by fashion photography for a while, but I realized that what really interested me was the world of beauty, as I explained to Susan Train.

"Very simple," she told me. "You have to meet Diana Vreeland. She happens to be staying at the Hôtel de Crillon right now. Off you go!"

I was a bit nervous, but I pulled myself together and went to her suite. She was sitting at her dressing table, applying cream to her face. Her hair was slicked back and very dark, and her eyes were just as dark—very piercing. She positively radiated charisma and natural authority despite her height—she was *tiny*. But she always appeared larger than life in photographs.

Diana barely looked at me and said, "Susan tells me you are interested in beauty . . . see, the cream I am using, it's not for you. You are too young for this kind of product."

Then she asked me about what I wanted to do, and I said that I was interested in the world of cosmetics and beauty products.

"Fine," she replied. "I am going to take care of you. Come to New York, and I will introduce you to the right people."

She was a visionary—and not just about fashion and beauty. As you already know, I learned from her and Susan Train, her fashion editor in France, that "impossible" was never an acceptable response. We always had to find solutions to all the requests that came to us from American *Vogue*, and no one ever wanted to let Diana down.

Eventually, the natural trend became the more popular one; it looked less sophisticated, but of course it still took work and skill to make a natural, "no-makeup" makeup look seem fresh and glowing. It's much easier to get that more natural yet finessed look now thanks to fabulous textures and the creation of unique colors in many different brands of makeup.

Even the French Make Beauty Mistakes!

While French women might love their beauty routines and have confidence in what they do and use, we still make mistakes. These are my favorite anecdotes that some friends kindly shared with me:

♥ One thing I will never try again is to use coconut oil on my face in wintertime. Although it's amazing in the summer, in the winter, coconut oil turns solid with the cold temperature. It really irritated my skin.

♥ When I am breaking out, I have a terrible habit of touching my face too much. It definitely makes things worse.

♥ I will never again do my own hair color alone at home.

♥ I will never apply self-tanner on my sister's legs again, as I once did a poor job and she was so upset!

♥ I will now avoid tanning too much and too fast, since the last time I did, I ended up looking like a cooked lobster—and that's before I started to peel!

♥ I will never again use sand at the beach as a body scrub. It produced a bad reaction, like a rough rash, which was a disaster given that I had only packed light dresses for the summer weather.

Part Two

Le Visage

Chapter 2

Beautiful Skin
at Any Age

I always compare skin to your favorite silk blouse. If you have some imperfections in your silk blouse, it should always be treated with delicate attention.

—HOLISTIC FACIALIST ISABELLE BELLIS

*A*mong the first beauty products I ever used were my face cleanser and toner. I can still close my eyes and remember the Shiseido Pureness Cleansing Gel in its light blue bottle. Or the Onagrine scrub that came in a round jar (back when I still used scrubs on my teenage skin). Every night, as I carefully applied and gently washed off these products, my mother's admonition to always go to bed with a clean face would be ringing in my ears.

Decades later, like most French women, I'm still obsessed with what cleansers work the best. What better way to show off your skin than with a stellar cleansing regimen the French way? Proper cleansing will not only undo damage from environmental assaults, but it will help slow down the natural aging process.

SIMPLE RULES: BASIC ROUTINE

One of the wonderful things about living in New York is that, believe it or not, my skin is much less dirty at the end of the day than it is when I'm in Paris. Manhattan is, after all, an island, surrounded by water, and there is often a breeze that freshens the air and minimizes pollution. Paris, on the other hand, can have terrible days of gray pollution that literally deposits itself under my nails.

Despite the cleaner air here, one thing that struck me when I moved to America is how unpopular facial cleansing is. I asked many different women in New York about this, and they all told me that one of the problems is that they started paying attention to face-cleansing when they were teenagers with acne, and the products they used were medicated and often smelled harsh and felt harsh, too. They weren't thinking about anything other than effectiveness, so there was no joy in the process.

I hope after reading this chapter that I will have convinced you to change your cleansing routine, because it's absolutely the most important step you can take to improve and maintain the health and vitality of your skin. I discussed this with Elisabeth Bouhadana, Global Scientific Communications Director at L'Oréal Paris International, to help you understand why:

♥ Daily skin hygiene means cleaning your skin very well, especially in the evening, to get rid of all the residues, dust, and pollution. The topmost layer of skin is made up of dead skin cells that form a protective barrier over the layers underneath, and this is the ideal condition to make dirt and grime stick, leading to clogged pores and inflammation.

- ♥ It is also where we find makeup residue, especially if you use an oil-based foundation every day. These oils are going to interact with your skin's natural oils (called sebum) and oxidize, which is another cause of troubled skin as well as a contributor to skin aging.
- ♥ If your skin is not clean, your moisturizer or serums will not be able to penetrate as well through a barrier made of sebum, dead cells, and product residues—even if it is the best moisturizer in the world! A clean face will optimize the benefits of all the skincare products you apply after being washed, whether serums, moisturizers, or anti-aging treatments.

Here is what I learned from French-born Terry de Gunzburg, founder of the skincare and makeup line By Terry (she is something of a legend among those in the French beauty world as the genius behind the creation of YSL's magical concealer, Touche Éclat): "Use that time for yourself. Think of your cleansing ritual as a bit of calming meditation, as something that will not only feel good and smell even better but leave your skin soft, dewy, and glowing. Find products that you love, with scents that transport you into these special moments of total relaxation. It is very easy to make those few moments when you remove your makeup and then wash up deeply pleasurable."

Terry de Gunzburg is also a fan of mixing several different makeup removers together. She explained why on an especially cold winter day in New York City, with a snowstorm in the forecast. We sat in the private room of a trendy little Upper East Side restaurant and talked so much that we didn't realize hours had passed and several inches of snow had already accumulated by the time we finished our meeting. Like a true French woman,

Terry merely smiled, shrugged, and went out into the snow in her chic winter coat and heels, and a taxi magically appeared.

"The key word is *purity*," she told me. "Makeup removal should be a daily routine. I love to mix three makeup removers together. I apply them one by one, by layer, and I massage the skin for three minutes. These are the three minutes I dedicate to myself! It's a relaxing time. I rinse well and with a lot of water. Then I apply a toner by hand. *Voilà!* My skin already has that glow."

Cleansing Products, Defined

There are countless different cleansers, and all of them fall into specific categories depending on their ingredients, textures, and purpose. Romain Gaillard, the French cofounder of US-based Detox Market store and e-shop, explains what they are for:

- ♥ Milk cleanser: Gentle, nourishing, and soothing, milk cleansers are classically recommended for dry or sensitive skin, and those made with plant oils are perfect for removing makeup and balancing all skin types—even oily.
- ♥ Foaming cleanser: Foaming cleansers have a very light feel and are fun to use but can be quite drying, so they're better for younger teen skin and those with oily skin. Even the gentlest foaming cleansers can be too harsh for those with dry or irritated skin, as the foam usually comes from sulfates—the same surfactants used in laundry and dish detergent.
- ♥ Cleansing gel: A gel cleanser is usually oil-based, which makes it good for removing makeup as well as grime.

♥ Cleansing oil: Oil cleansers don't make your skin oilier! They are rich formulas ideal for dry skin and for those who want to avoid tugging or pulling on their skin when removing makeup. For the double cleansing method (which you'll read about on page 34) try using an oil cleanser first, and then continue with a more traditional face wash using a gel or cleansing milk, as oil cleansers can have the tendency to linger on your skin's surface.

♥ Eye makeup remover: This can be an oil- or water-based cleanser that is gentle enough to be used on the sensitive eye area without causing any stinging or tenderness. Oil-based removers tend to be more effective at wiping away eye shadow and mascara. The choice of a good-quality cotton pad is as important as the choice of a good eye makeup remover.

♥ Toner: Toner has gotten a bad rap for being either unnecessary or overly harsh, but it's actually an essential step provided you're using the right one. Modern, natural toners use plant essences to deliver targeted ingredients deep into the skin. Prepping with toner ensures your serums and moisturizers absorb effectively. You can also use them to set makeup or to refresh the skin throughout the day.

♥ Micellar water: Micellar waters were invented in the 1990s for Parisian women to save their skin from the region's notoriously harsh tap water. A micellar water is comprised of micelles (tiny cleansing oil molecules) suspended in water. The idea is that you can saturate a cotton pad and sweep away makeup without needing to rinse. The micelles and cotton act like a magnet for impurities. A micellar water is more of a makeup remover and shouldn't replace your regular cleanser.

Don't Bring Eye Makeup into Bed with You

Start with your eyes, because your eye shadow, liner, and mascara tend to be heavily pigmented and more difficult to remove than what's on other parts of your face. Be gentle! Always use soft and highly absorbent cotton pads, as tissues can be too abrasive for the delicate skin of your eyelids and around your eyes.

I like to use an oil-based eye makeup remover, as it hydrates while it works. When you cleanse your face, any leftover residue will be washed away. The other key rule is to be generous with how much of the remover you use, as getting all the makeup off (especially mascara) is so much easier when your cotton pad is damp rather than dry. Leave the pad on your eye for a few seconds so that the product has time to impregnate the mascara to fully remove it.

Our Favorite Eye Makeup Removers

For All Ages: Chanel, Kiehl's, Klorane, Lancôme, Make Up For Ever, Bioderma, M·A·C Pro Eye Makeup Remover, Saje Natural Wellness Herbal Balm.

Double Cleansing Is the Way to Go

I learned about double cleansing from two of the best-known facialists in Paris. The first is Joëlle Ciocco, also known as the Queen of Beauty. Her sophisticated and upscale beauty center in the heart of Paris's *très* chic Madeleine district is one of the most sought-after *rendez-vous* in the city for women from all over the world. (I was a little nervous before we met, but she was so incredibly warm and lovely that I understood why she has had such a strong following for so many years.) The second holistic facialist, Isabelle Bellis, who was trained by Joëlle and who specializes in natural ingredients, has enviable skin and the most gracious way of moving like a ballerina. Isabelle taught me the importance of facial massage to improve circulation and the flow of oxygen to the tissues. Use this cleansing technique and your skin will reap the benefits:

- Good hygiene does not mean burning your skin. It means respecting it. So you need to clean your skin thoroughly at night, while respecting the flora of your skin. If you feel "squeaky clean," have rough or dry patches on your skin, or feel as though your skin isn't balanced, your cleanser is much too harsh.

- In fact, you need to clean your face and neck *twice*. The first time, you get rid of the impurities, pollution, or makeup with a creamy product.

- The second time, you clean the topmost layer, or the stratum corneum, itself. When you do this, you optimize the skin's natural protection and regeneration, which primarily take place at night while you're sleeping.

- It's best to do this gently, or you can end up with dry and irritated skin.

- Cleansing milks or cleansing oils are best for dry skin.

- After the double cleansing, apply your favorite toner

with a cotton pad. Do not rinse. You can use a spray of thermal spring water, such as the ones from Avène or Evian, and blot off or wipe off gently with tissues.

▼ A quick, gentle wash in the morning with a toner or a lightweight cleanser will remove any impurities. Make sure to rinse it with a spray of thermal water as you do at night.

▼ You can use products from the same brand, or mix them according to your taste and sensitivity.

Cleansing Your Face without Water

Delphine Prudhomme, manager of the Françoise Morice Beauty Institute in Paris, taught me the most effective way to do this. No matter the age, the technique remains the same, and it leaves your skin soft, without any feeling of tightness:

▼ At night, first use a milky makeup-removing lotion on a cotton pad in small circular movements to get rid of impurities and makeup. One cotton pad should suffice.

▼ Then, you must use several cotton pads with a soft cleansing lotion until the last cotton is perfectly white after use. If you have makeup on, you might need at least three or four cotton pads. It is preferable to use hydrophilic cotton, as it's softer and more absorbent.

▼ In the morning, you will only need to use one cotton pad with lotion on it.

▼ Always dry your skin well before applying any serums or moisturizers.

My Favorite Way to Cleanse My Face

I listened to these experts and now follow the cleansing-twice rule, and I've found that it has really improved the quality and glow of my skin. Who knew that something as mundane as cleansing could become one of those keys to the healthiest possible skin? This is what I do at the end of the day:

- First I remove all my makeup with a cleansing milk or oil, the texture of which is so comfortable that it really "invites" the massage.

- If I feel that I had more makeup on than usual or that the city was more polluted than usual, I follow the Clarins technique: I warm the cleanser in the palm of my hands, then apply it to my face and start to lift off my hands, creating a suction effect that removes impurities.

- I sometimes also use a popular and wonderful little electronic cleansing device that can be found in department stores or online, the Foreo Luna Mini. It's made with a silicone brush that has soft touch points that gently vibrate, leaving your skin very clean and supple afterward. I dampen my skin, apply my choice of cleanser, and then massage it in with the Luna.

- Next, I rinse with warm water, using a special glove. I still use the very French *gant de toilette,* which I cannot find in the United States! It is a piece of terry cloth made so you can put your hand inside it, like a glove. If you are looking for something similar, a soft face towel or terry cloth can be used. I leave it a few seconds under warm water and then use it to wipe my face and neck.

♥ I follow this with a second cleansing, using a rich product such as a cleansing milk, and I rinse again with my wet terry cloth.

♥ I pat my skin dry and then use a cotton pad to apply a toner. I always try to remember to swipe the front and back of my neck, as well as my décolleté.

♥ Nice cotton pads make such a difference. I have become very particular about them, and when I find a brand I like I stock up with a few bags! I never travel without my cotton pads because they really are the key part to a perfect face cleansing.

♥ Finally, I add a spritz of Avène or La Roche-Posay thermal spring water. This doesn't need to be rinsed off.

♥ In the morning, I find that I don't need to use a cleanser—just use a bit of toner on a cotton pad followed by some thermal water to remove impurities accumulated during the night and to reset my skin.

This may sound like a lot, but it really isn't. It just takes a few minutes and leaves my face ultraclean, hydrated, and super dewy. I've got the glow. Even better, I wake up with the glow, too!

Our Favorite Cleansers

These are brands I'm sure you know and use already, as well as some new ones I think are soon to become your new favorites. These cleansers have different textures for all skin types.

Jeunesse: Avène, Clinique, Dermalogica, Clarins, Osmia Organics Rose Clay Facial Soap.

Plénitude: Joëlle Ciocco Lait Onctueux Capital, Pai Camellia & Rose Gentle Hydrating Cleanser, Kiehl's Midnight Recovery Botanical Cleansing Oil, de Mamiel Restorative Cleansing Balm, Caudalie Make-up Removing Cleansing Oil, Alexandra Soveral Angel Balm, Tata Harper Nourishing Oil Cleanser.

Maturité: Biologique Recherche Lait E.V., Caudalie Gentle Cleansing Milk, Clarins Total Cleansing Oil, Estée Lauder Advanced Night Micro Cleansing Balm, Shu Uemura Cleansing Oils, Joëlle Ciocco Sensitive Cleansing Milk.

Our Favorite Toners

Toners help ensure that your skin is perfectly clean without stripping away natural oils. When you use them on a cotton pad, you'll know you're done when the cotton pad stays white after use. This is an especially useful step for *jeunesse*, particularly if you have oily skin and use a cleansing foam that may leave a feeling of tightness.

Jeunesse: L'Oréal, Bioderma Micellar Water.

Plénitude: Avène Gentle Toning Lotion, Clarins, Caudalie Moisturizing Toner, Tammy Fender Essential C Tonic.

Maturité: Orlane B21 Lotion Extraordinaire, Joëlle Ciocco Perfective Lotion, Filorga Anti-Ageing Micellar Solution.

USE YOUR CLEANSING ROUTINE TO
BRIGHTEN A SLUGGISH COMPLEXION

I've noticed that the drugstore shelves in America are loaded with scrubs and exfoliants—and French *pharmacies* are not. We are just not raised with the notion that the only way to get clean skin is by scrubbing it. In fact, one of the worst things you can do for your skin is to scrub it too harshly and too often. According to skin expert Philippe Simonin, using harsh scrubs or dermabrasion is like "removing the roof of the house." Scrubbing doesn't make your skin cleaner; using a good cleanser is all that's needed to remove the grime of the day, even if you have acne or oily skin.

If you miss your scrubs, simply switch to a gentle exfoliating cleanser. The key word is *gentle*. If you still need more of a glow, add a brightening treatment. (An added bonus is that a brightener will even out any pigmentation issues.) A French woman would never use a harsh scrub or attempt a chemical peel at home. "Every time you do a peel, there is a microtrauma," explains Philippe. "If you were to do a scrub only once—yes, *once*!—you would take off three layers of skin. It takes forty-eight hours to rebuild one layer of skin. It takes a week to recover."

Our Favorite Gentle Exfoliators and Brighteners
Cleansing Exfoliators: Aurelia Refine & Polish Miracle Balm, Dior Hydra Life Time to Glow Ultra Fine Exfoliating Powder, Filorga Scrub & Glow Reoxygenating Exfoliating Mask, Omorovicza Thermal Cleansing Balm.

Brighteners: Caudalie Vinoperfect Radiance Serum, Natura Bissé Diamond White Glowing Mask, Osmia Organics Brighten Facial Serum, Tata Harper Concentrated Brightening Serum.

Use Masks for Deep Cleansing and to Banish Dull Skin

Masks are also a great way to deep-cleanse and brighten a sluggish complexion, so look for those with words and phrases like *brightening* or *even out your skin tone* on the label. Whenever I use a mask, which isn't often enough, I always find it extremely pleasant, especially as they make you slow down and relax while they're on. I know I need to do them more often. Just not when anyone can see me—especially with sheet masks, as I think that would terrify my children!

Our Favorite Masks

For younger skin that needs a detox effect, clay masks will help with excess oil and impurities. Try Biotherm, Captain Blankenship Mermaid Detox Face Mask, Dior Hydra Life Pores Away Pink Clay Mask, Kiehl's, Kypris Deep Forest Clay, and Odacité Synergie[4] Immediate Skin Perfecting Beauty Masque.

For hydration and brightness: Avène Tolérance Extrême Mask, Pai Rosehip BioRegenerate Rapid Radiance Mask, and Tata Harper Resurfacing Mask.

For a wow effect, try these sheet masks: Amore Pacific, Estée Lauder Advanced Night Repair Concentrated Recovery PowerFoil Mask, and Shiseido Benefiance.

TREATING ACNE

Proper cleansing is key to dealing with acne. French mothers teach their daughters to start cleaning their faces before they are teenagers, explaining that it helps to clear pores to remove the oil and bacteria that cause blemishes to form. My mother taught me that; she remembers trying out different purifying masks when she was only fourteen! Visits to a dermatologist are also part of our regular routine, just like seeing a dentist, not only to prevent or cure acne but also to have a thorough check of any pigmented brown spots linked to sun exposure.

For All Ages

Acne is not caused by a French woman's beloved chocolate or by the French fries she eats when she orders a *steak frites*. It's caused by a combination of factors, primarily hormonal and due to oil production and the *P. acnes* bacteria, which is why all types of women can suffer from it, from fifteen-year-olds to women who've just given birth, or even women *d'un certain âge*.

In fact, as skincare expert Philippe Simonin explains, "Mothers would run away when I said to their children that acne is linked to ten causes: four-tenths hereditary, three-tenths hormonal, one-tenth due to nervousness and stress, one-tenth dietary, and one-tenth due to the sun. How can we tell a young person to not be stressed, to eat normally, and to be careful in regard to this and that? We can't!"

Jeunesse

French teenagers rarely self-treat if they have acne—they hurry to the pharmacist or dermatologist for expert advice.

According to Paris-based endocrinologist Dr. Catherine Brémont-Weill and dermatologist Dr. Sophie Laglenne, most teenagers have acne, and it does have an impact on their life. It is a serious issue, as acne rarely goes away on its own. Whether the pimples, blackheads, and marks are highly visible or not, a consultation with the dermatologist is recommended, with follow-up if needed.

- Daily cleansing with acne-treatment products (noncomedogenic, in particular) is a must, but this might not have a long-term effect on stubborn acne.
- Sun exposure is not a solution, as the sun is the "devil in disguise." Though a tan can hide redness and pimples, it damages the skin and can actually cause more pimples to form.
- Early treatment decreases the risk of permanent scars, especially for cystic acne (very large pimples that are tempting to pick). Here are some of the most common treatments that might be done by a dermatologist:
  - Topical treatments such as retinoids, fruit acids, azelaic acid, benzoyl peroxide, topical antibiotics.
  - Oral treatments: Antibiotics, zinc gluconate, and sometimes isotretinoin (Accutane) for severe cases that could be resistant to the previous treatments, but Accutane mandates strict medical care because of possible strong side effects, and it can never be taken if you are considering getting pregnant.

♡ Laser and light treatments are sometimes used for pimples or scars.

♡ Anti-androgen hormone treatments can sometimes be an option. They must be discussed on a case-by-case basis with a medical professional.

In general, always clean your face before going to bed. No scrubs or scrubbing, please! Try to follow as balanced a diet as possible. Avoid fried food, processed food, and too many animal proteins. Reduce spicy foods, too. According to renowned nutritionist and functional medicine expert Dr. Georges Mouton, "Spicy food can cause irritation quite easily. If it burns in your mouth, it's going to burn your intestine, and thus we're talking about something that will harm the skin. Skin will be inflamed because the intestine is inflamed."

Ask a nutritionist, if needed, for additional advice. I know it is easier said than done, but it is worth trying!

Plénitude

Acne during these decades is almost always hormonally triggered—sometimes women in their twenties can suddenly develop acne for the first time in their lives, or during or after a pregnancy, or during perimenopause, when the female hormones begin to decline. Discuss this with your gynecologist or dermatologist.

Often, though, acne at this age may be a simple case of contact dermatitis, which can be caused by a new detergent or soap, or an allergy to something benign. Change to gentle, fragrance-free products designed for sensitive skin. Keep your face clean. If you do get any blackheads near your nose, pore strips usually do the trick of removing them.

Maturité

As with *plénitude*, if you suddenly develop acne, you should see a physician right away, as it is a sign that there might be hormonal imbalances, which are rare at this age. Better safe than sorry!

Our Favorite Acne Products

For All Ages: Avène Cleanance Expert, Bioderma, La Roche-Posay, Osmia Organics Black Clay Facial Soap, Odacité Black Cumin+Cajeput Serum Concentrate.

Pharmacist Claire Bausset recommends these products: Alternate morning and evening with Bioderma Sébium H20 for the face, using a cotton pad, and Bioderma Sébium Purifying Cleansing Foaming Gel for the shower. During the day, use treatment cream SVR Lysalpha, which has an SPF of 50. In the evening, apply La Roche-Posay Effaclar Duo, which will quickly reduce severe imperfections and prevent spots from forming while smoothing the complexion.

Chapter 3

Hydration: Improving Your Daily Beauty Routine

Every woman can be beautiful.

—ESTÉE LAUDER

*E*stée was right. Every woman *can* be beautiful, but it does require a little time and dedication.

For years I used to love these cute little freckles that would suddenly pop up on my cheekbones and my nose in the middle of sunny summers. They were the result of a good tan, I thought, when actually, every one of those "cute" little freckles was a visible reminder of the damage I was unknowingly inflicting on my skin. They're brown spots, which I much prefer to avoid!

So while I can't turn back the clock and decide that freckles weren't so cute after all, I can take the best possible care of my skin now, because the aging process is inevitable and inexorable. Understanding what happens as you get older is the first step toward devising a skincare plan that will be the most effective for your own unique needs.

SKIN AGING IS INEVITABLE

French women know that the earlier you start a comprehensive skincare regimen, the more youthful your skin will remain. Still, no matter what you do, as you get older your skin will thin, lose elasticity, and begin to sag. Its power to regenerate as well as its oil production diminishes, leaving your skin much drier and prone to wrinkling.

Overall Aging

The skin has three layers: the epidermis, the outermost layer; the dermis, the middle layer; and the hypodermis, the very bottom. If you look at the skin like a succession of layers, like a bed, then the hypodermis would be the very bottom of the frame, with its cushioning fat cells; the dermis would be the frame, with the fibers of its collagen and elastin (the proteins that comprise skin cells); then there is the mattress, the epidermis, which is constantly renewing itself. The most hydrated compartment is the dermis, which is composed of 80 percent water, and it is constantly losing water as it filtrates up toward the less-hydrated epidermis. Skin cells are formed in the deeper layers and migrate upward, where they acquire different properties and finally die as they reach the surface, called the stratum corneum.

We will always have some hydration in the skin because, at the cellular level, our bodies are largely comprised of water, which is what keeps skin dewy and supple, even well into your nineties. Over time, however, the collagen fibers begin to degrade due to the penetration of the damaging UVA and UVB rays. Thanks to Elisabeth Bouhadana, I now understand the skin's aging process. Here is some key information:

Jeunesse

In your twenties, your skin is soft and well hydrated and regenerates quickly—skin cells have a very short life span, usually about three to four weeks at this stage. They push up from the lower skin layers and end up on your stratum corneum, or the very topmost layer.

This is, however, the decade when your skin is slowly starting to change. From a biological standpoint, the first sign of aging is the skin's decreased capacity for retaining water in its structure. Stored in the top two skin layers, the dermis and the epidermis, is a natural spongelike substance called hyaluronic acid, designed to keep moisture in. Over time, the skin cells that produce the hyaluronic acid lose some of their capacity to retain water. Hyaluronic acid can also be damaged by the environment, pollution, UV rays from the sun, and oxidizing agents. When this happens, these cells will not be able to retain as much moisture, and your skin will gradually become drier.

In addition, fine wrinkles might start to appear, but they are still barely visible; it's more like a feeling of the skin being less supple or having slightly less radiance.

Unfortunately, you can still get acne at this age, even if you didn't have it as a teenager, and it should be treated (no picking, please!) to avoid scarring.

What to Do

Take advantage of your young age to start good skincare habits. As you reach your late teens and early twenties, your priority is to keep your face clean, so now is the time to make a proper washup part of your daily routine. It's just as essential as brushing your teeth, except that it is a lot more pleasant once you start using wonderful products that smell good and make you feel better.

Be gentle in the way you treat your skin. Harsh scrubs should never be used—you don't need them, and they can damage your skin. If you get blemishes, do *not* scrub them, which paradoxically will make your skin much worse, as you already learned in the acne section on page 42. If you use peels, follow the directions and don't overuse them. Overzealous cleansing actually leads to more oil production, which can lead to acne and clogged pores. As facialist Joëlle Ciocco explains, "I have seen abuse and abrasion of the skin due to the use of the wrong products that are so aggressive that they contribute to skin aging rather than helping it. Why would you burn, dry, and peel? Rather than nourishing and maintaining healthy skin, the overuse of these wrong products expedites the skin's aging process."

It is no longer "no pain, no gain"; gentle is the new way to go.

You should also use sunscreen every day that you're going to be out in the sun, and try to follow a healthy diet as much as you can.

Plénitude

When you reach your thirties and forties, different factors are going to be affecting your skin as it irrevocably starts to change and becomes more fragile. Small lines and wrinkles start to appear.

You might notice that your skin often becomes drier and is more sensitive to changes of temperature (between air conditioning and the outdoors, for example, or during the change of seasons). Your face will show the effects more if you are lacking sleep or if you had too much to drink!

LORRAINE: I remember when I turned fifty, my dermatologist told me that I had had my "quota" of sun and that I needed to pay more attention to how sensitive the skin on my décolleté had become. Right now, it's one of my priorities to not only protect it but cover it completely. On vacation, I still love going to the beach, but I will not lounge for hours in the sun anymore, and certainly not unprotected. I love the sun too much to stay out of it entirely, but I know that my skin will age more quickly if I don't take preventative measures. One needs to come to terms with time; you get more wrinkles as you age, but you get an overall softness, too. There is a balance that happens, and age brings you more wisdom while teaching you to enjoy each moment more fully. One needs to learn to take advantage of the best of these beauty stages, keeping in mind that what makes you beautiful will always remain.

What to Do

This is the time to change your cleansing routine, adapting it so that you use products that are more hydrating. Whether your skin is oily or dry, the cleansing/exfoliating foams or the drying lotions of your teens and twenties are no longer an option. It is a good time to start regular treatments like the facial massage you'll learn about on page 88 to maintain the tonicity and elasticity of the face. It is also the time to be extra diligent about protecting your skin from the sun. If you are going to be exposed to the sun, then remember to not leave the house without having first applied a product with SPF, or a broad-spectrum sunscreen.

Maturité

We all have to deal with issues linked to menopause, usually around the age of fifty or so, although perimenopause often starts when a woman is in her late forties. Not only will you *feel* the effects, but they *show*—skin becomes drier, visibly so; wrinkles become more pronounced; and there is an even more pronounced loss of elasticity that leads to drooping and sagging.

> **RÉGINE:** I will never forget a vacation we took in Portugal. The weather was gorgeous; it was sunny every day, but extremely windy as well. Never before had I seen my face so marked by the sun because the mixture of the wind with the salty seawater and the strong rays of the sun was a really bad cocktail. My skin paid a hard price, and it took a long time to recover.

What to Do

Before you do anything to your skin, see your gynecologist to have your hormones measured, and then discuss the pros and cons of hormone replacement therapy to see if it's an option for you. Next, see a dermatologist to discuss more intensive prescription-only products and/or treatments. Now is not the time to self-diagnose! Then, try to minimize environmental factors that affect your skin, such as sun exposure, air pollution, and cigarettes. Be active. Sleep well. You still need sunscreen, good food, and lots of love!

Be Aware of Hormonal Changes

I discussed the effect of diminishing hormonal levels with renowned Parisian endocrinologist Dr. Catherine Brémont-Weill:

Most hormones have a role in skin regeneration, in particular the thyroid hormones, the sex hormones (estrogen, progesterone, and androgens), growth hormones, and melatonin (which helps regulate sleep). Hormonal fluctuations, whether they're physiological (puberty, menopause) or the side effect of an illness (excessive or insufficient production) or linked to a lifestyle (stress, lack of sleep), all have an effect on the skin.

During perimenopause and menopause, when a woman's hormonal production slows down, skin-protective estrogen levels drop considerably. This leads to a decrease in hydration and a decrease in the production of collagen fibers. The skin becomes less toned and less supple as well as thinner and drier. In addition, many women have undiagnosed or undertreated hypothyroidism (not enough of the thyroid hormones that regulate your metabolism), which often leaves the skin dry, pale, and yellowish and can even thicken it, sometimes creating swelling.

Anti-aging creams can prove useful in reducing the visible effects of hormonal changes during menopause. For example, retinoids (vitamin-A acid, retinol, retinaldehyde) and fruit acids are useful to smooth the superficial layers; retinoids also stimulate the deeper skin layers. Antioxidant-based creams (such as vitamin C, vitamin E, carotenoids, resveratrol, and polyphenols, for example) decrease the harmful effects that pro-oxidant substances (linked to the environment, in particular the sun) can have on the skin. Other ingredients to look for include glycerols, essential fatty acids, hyaluronic acid, and ceramides.

ALWAYS PROTECT YOUR SKIN: HYDRATION

Moisturizing is not the same for all women. Nor is protection. Each woman must learn to identify her skin type before she chooses her skincare.

—HELENA RUBINSTEIN

No matter your age, normal water loss is an ongoing process, so you need to keep your skin hydrated for it to stay supple. A good hydrating moisturizer is an essential part of your skincare regimen.

Whatever your needs, read on to find out much more about how the French protect their skin.

Moisturizing Products, Defined

Skincare products for moisture each have a specific purpose. It helps to know how to navigate the variety of choices so you don't waste money on any items you don't need.

- ♥ Moisturizers: A moisturizing lotion or cream is an emulsified oil. It provides more of a barrier function and locks moisture into the skin.
- ♥ Wrinkle/Firming Cream: A wrinkle or firming cream can be moisturizing, but it will also have active ingredients with a firming or smoothing effect to minimize the appearance of fine lines.
- ♥ Dry Oils: A dry oil might sound like an oxymoron, but it's the name for a lightweight oil that absorbs easily. The feel of an oil has to do with its unique ratios of omega fatty acids, with dry oils being very high in

omega-6 (linoleic acid). These include grapeseed oil, prickly pear oil, argan oil, and rosehip oil. Interestingly, a recent study showed that people with acne tend to have low levels of linoleic acid, causing their sebum to be too sticky. This explains why a dry oil can actually balance the skin even if you are oily.

♥ Serums: Serums have a higher concentration of active ingredients and usually have a specific purpose. They tend to be lighter in texture than moisturizers but are still more potent and nourishing. For more, see the serums section on page 61.

♥ Hydrating Toner or Essence: A hydrating toner or essence is a useful step after cleansing and before applying a serum and/or moisturizer, as it adds another layer of moisture. You can apply it with a cotton pad or just sprinkle a little bit into your hands and gently pat it all over your skin.

♥ Thermal Water Spray: Thermal waters are incredible for the skin. Found deep underground, they're mineral-rich, naturally devoid of bacteria and pollutants, and are exceptionally soft, leaving a soothing, protective film on the skin. The water sources have unique components, such as specific minerals, which assist the skin in different ways. They are the perfect way to finish your cleansing routine in the morning and evening.

♥ Masks: According to the Detox Market's cofounder Romain Gaillard, "The difference between good skin and great skin is masking. Doing an intensive treatment at least once a week takes your skincare routine to the next level. A moisturizing mask provides intense nourishment to bring the bounce and plumpness back to skin. Clay and charcoal masks are good for drawing out impurities; brightening masks can even out skin tone and minimize brown spots. Sheet masks are serum-infused, face-shaped pieces of paper with holes for eyes, nose, and mouth that are applied to the face and left on for about ten minutes. They come individually wrapped and are handy for travel. Sheet masks are thought to be more effective than cream masks because they are saturated with concentrated skincare ingredients. You need to lie down and relax when you're using one to keep the mask in place so the serum has time to absorb."

HYDRATING YOUR FACE

People need to understand that some treatments can only show their true effectiveness over time. With their cream they want immediate effect, but understand that some treatments will only work over the long term. We need to act on both.

—ODILE MOHEN, CONSUMER AND MARKET INSIGHT GLOBAL
DIRECTOR—L'ORÉAL RESEARCH AND INNOVATION

In addition to the facialists and aestheticians beloved by French women, we also adore our neighborhood *pharmacies,* as you know. The pharmacists are trained differently in France and have a much deeper knowledge of skincare and over-the-counter treatments than a salesclerk at a big-box American store, so from a very young age, we know that we can always go to our local pharmacist for expert advice and recommendations regarding which cream is the most hydrating, the most adapted for our skin type, or the best to treat conditions like acne or dryness. Having someone so close to home certainly helps to build good habits, and now that I live in America, I tell my friends here to find a dermatologist they trust for advice or to seek out an aesthetician in a spa or salon who offers treatments that they like. They'll do!

Thanks to my mother's knowledge on this topic, hydration has been a part of my skincare routine since I was a teenager. At the time, I would alternate between a light moisturizer containing ingredients to treat acne, recommended by my pharmacist or dermatologist, and over-the-counter products that caught my attention on the shelves of my neighborhood beauty stores. My friends and I would spend hours debating which brand to choose, because the French skincare brands were pretty savvy when it came to marketing their newest potions to teenagers, often counting on the fact that the packaging was often more enticing than the boring ingredients list!

Jeunesse

Even if your skin is oily, you still need a moisturizer. Treatment products designed to combat excess oil or acne often dry out oily skin. Your skin then senses that it's getting dry, so it actually steps up oil production, which begins an endless cycle of intermittent oily and dry skin—sometimes both at once, leaving you with dry patches on your cheeks and an oily forehead.

What to Do

When searching for a moisturizer, look for products that are oil-free, noncomedogenic (non–pore clogging), and lightweight.

Avoid pore-clogging ingredients like petrolatum, as they are too heavy for your skin.

Products We Love

♥ Depending on your skin type/condition (to treat acne, for dry skin) you may want a light cream from Avène, Bioderma, Embryolisse, La Roche-Posay, Nuxe, or Dior Hydra Life Sorbet Creme.

♥ If you like all-in-one products, try BB (blemish balm) or CC (color correction) creams. They give you moisturizing benefits in addition to a tint/more opaque finish, and often an SPF, too. Try La Roche-Posay Effaclar BB Blur or Erborian CC Crème.

♥ I also like Osmia Organics Purely Simple Face Cream, which has an aloe base that is good for sensitive skin, and Vintner's Daughter, an excellent dry oil.

♥ At night, you may not always need to add a moisturizer if your skin has been perfectly cleaned and toned.

Plénitude

When you reach your mid-thirties, you want more moisture and creams that will also keep your natural glow.

What to Do

Keep your routine simple with a day cream applied directly on the skin or on top of a serum.

This is also a good time to start using masks, which have a fast-acting potency that ensures results. Serum-infused sheet masks are extremely easy to use and clean up. If it's hot out, or if it's wintertime and your home has dry heat, try refrigerating the mask first, as it will instantly provide a cooling effect when applied.

Why are moisturizers so important during *plénitude*? Around thirty-five years of age, the dehydration lines have settled and cannot be erased even with good hydration. We can still use creams with biological and mechanical properties to combat this reaction.

Biological products will stimulate the production of collagen, but you can also visually hide lines in a mechanical way. How? By *filling* them. Imagine a brick wall. Once in a while you can use caulking to fill the gaps between the bricks. The same thing can be done with the skin by using a cream that will fill the lines. Even though it won't be permanent, it can last for one day. You apply the cream, wash it off at night, and then reapply the next day.

Products We Love

Filorga's serum is ideal before applying makeup. Depending on the season, I may want a richer cream. Some of my favorites are Avène Rich Compensating Cream, Clinique Moisture Surge, Caudalie Face Lifting Soft Cream, Clarins Multi-Active or Extra-Firming Day Cream, and Estée Lauder Revitalizing Supreme+ Global Anti-Aging Wake Up Balm. A lighter version for the summer such as Filorga Hydra-Filler Pro-Youth Boosting Moisturizer is a good choice. A great discovery for the sunny summer months is to use SkinCeuticals Physical Matte UV Defense SPF 50.

Maturité

RÉGINE: Carita was a pioneer in creating amazing textures in their facial moisturizers. They were incredibly light, not heavy or thick at all, making them an ideal base for makeup. They came in little vials.

What to Do

After turning fifty, you will likely want to add more deeply hydrating products into your routine. You may need to be patient before you see long-lasting results. As Elisabeth Bouhadana explains, "Cosmetics are actually able to correct hydration, and some of them work instantly. They can be anti-wrinkle, too, as long as they have soft-focus pigments, firming components, and active ingredients that can blur the lines. These are little tricks that do the job instantly, and they give the active biological ingredients time to do their job in depth because they need to penetrate deeply into the layers of the epidermis to stimulate the skin cells there. It takes your skin at least twenty-one to twenty-eight days for the newly formed cells to reach the surface of the skin, and this process slows with age. Since the cream has an instant mechanical result, even if it is 'fake,' this gives you a better complexion while the product is also doing its work from within your cells."

In other words, while you can see immediate improvement from a moisturizer and/or wrinkle cream you're using, it usually takes at least a month to see deeper results.

Products We Love

LORRAINE: In the morning, I use C-Recover Anti-Fatigue Radiance Concentrate, an intensive vitamin-C radiance treatment from Filorga, followed by their Iso-Structure Absolute Firming Cream. I am also still faithful to Avène. To give my skin some radiance and youthfulness before a special evening, I use the ampoules by Ingrid Millet Perle de

Caviar Bio-Marine Extract. This is by far my best-kept skincare secret! I call them my "magic trick" because they give me a glow that I have never, ever found anywhere else, and they have saved my look more times than I can remember. I have been using them for almost forty years. They also help makeup stay on longer and better and magically remove traces of fatigue.

RÉGINE: I was very partial to Orlane products for a long time; they were very high quality, especially the B21 Lotion Extraordinaire. Now, I use either La Roche-Posay Substiane Visible Density and Volume Replenishing Moisturizer, Dior Prestige La Crème, or Caudalie.

What We Think About Supplements

LORRAINE: The French are big believers in supplements to complement topical skincare products, and even now I am like an antenna that tries to get all the best information on those that will have benefits on my skin, and I only test products that have been vouched for by medical experts with years of experience in skincare and in treating other medical conditions. I did a three-month trial of Dexsil Pharma Organic Silicium, a drinkable food supplement made with silica and nettle that has had a pretty miraculous effect on my skin, hair, and nails, making them stronger and thicker, as well as improving my joint flexibility and mobility. It was recommended by a chiropractor who saw its benefits in his patients.

RÉGINE: Only a few years ago, I started to complement my beauty and wellness routine with supplements, especially Coenzyme Q10 (or CoQ10). It is a vitamin-like antioxidant that cells use to generate energy. Your body makes it naturally, but levels start to diminish with age. That's one supplement that worked really well for me.

Whatever you choose, don't self-diagnose or think that a supplement that worked for a friend might have the same effect for you, because your body's chemistry and micronutrient needs are unique to you. If you think you have any vitamin or mineral deficiencies, visit your physician for a blood test to obtain accurate levels for assessment.

USING SERUMS AND NIGHT CREAMS

Serums

Serums started to appear in the 1980s because there was a demand among women with an active lifestyle seeking a lighter, less heavy, yet still effective and highly concentrated product.

Serums are categorized according to their function. You can choose from an oil-based serum with repairing properties and many active ingredients; there are also choices for hydrating, firming, pore-reducing, brightening, evening out of the skin tone, and even single vitamin serums (like vitamin C) that can be mixed into other serums or your favorite moisturizer.

According to Elisabeth Bouhadana: You need the best possible carrier, and serums are really good carriers. What's more important is the *presence* of the active ingredients. For example, if you have a vitamin C cream with 20 percent vitamin C but it is not well formulated, you can apply it morning and night but it will do nothing. Vitamin C must be protected from oxidation and needs to penetrate the skin; to do that, the formulation must be specifically adapted to your needs.

For pharmaceutical serums, we look for biological components with the ability to penetrate, correct, and stimulate; with creams, we seek more protection, nutrition, hydration, and comfort. With a serum, we don't look for suppleness but instead make sure it leaves no residual product on the skin.

How to Apply Serums

Choose your serum according to your skincare needs. For example, you can use a brightening serum in the daytime (once your skin is dry from your morning cleansing routine) and a deeply nourishing one at night (after your full evening cleansing routine). A serum should always be applied on a clean face and *before* any other treatment product. If you apply it on top of a moisturizer, it won't be able to penetrate through the cream, and it will just be wasted!

My mother has been a devotee of Estée Lauder's Advanced Night Repair since its launch in 1982. The first product to contain hyaluronic acid, it had a huge effect on the skincare market—it may be hard to believe now, but it was pretty revolutionary and created an entirely new audience for advanced at-home skincare.

As for me, I like to use the Clarins method recommended by Prisca Courtin-Clarins, the granddaughter of Jacques Courtin-Clarins, founder of the Clarins cosmetic empire and the creator of this method. He believed that you should always treat your skin gently and softly. This is what to do: To apply the Clarins Double Serum, warm the product in the palm of your hands. Apply by patting the whole hand gently all over your face and neck. Then press your hands lightly on your face, starting at your chin and going up to your forehead. Finish by pressing gently on your neck. This way, you'll make sure all of the serum is absorbed.

Night Creams

Is it always necessary to choose special moisturizers or treatment creams that are designated for nighttime use? The answer is that you have to listen to how your skin feels. Often your skin doesn't feel dehydrated at the end of the day, especially after a cleansing milk or oil. If so, keep your skin *au naturel*! When your skin reaches its *maturité*, it may become more necessary to use a cream, as the skin will need that extra boost of moisture.

What I learned from all these experts is that, however tempting it may be, women don't need to use too many products. Using more doesn't mean greater efficiency. You need to start with one product—a basic moisturizer—and adjust as you go. When you see it working, you'll be more inclined to keep using it, and the longer you stick with a product that's good for your skin, the better it will work.

At night, depending on how my skin looks and feels, I either spritz it with thermal water and I'm done, or I moisturize both my face and neck with a night cream or dry oil. I take a good minute to apply the cream with a gentle massage around my eyes, and then on my face, starting at my jawline, massaging up to my cheeks and forehead, and finishing along my neck.

RÉGINE: After sixty-five years, my skin has gotten better by putting on nourishing creams at night. This is something that I never did for many years, because I liked sleeping without anything on my skin so it could breathe. My skin simply did not need extra hydration before bedtime, and it still looked rested the next day. However, my skin certainly needs more moisture now, and it feels suppler and almost like it's been ironed out every morning.

Products We Love

Tried-and-loved night creams: Clarins Extra-Firming Night or Multi-Active Nuit, Darphin Aromatic Renewing Balm, Nuxe Crème Fraiche, and Guerlain Midnight Secret. If you like the satin finish of oils, try Alexandra Soveral Midnight Oil, Aerin Rose de Grasse Oil, Marisa Berenson Fabulous Oil, Caudalie Overnight Recovery Oil, BioEffect EGF Serum, or Estée Lauder Advanced Night Repair.

Humidifying Your Home Is Good for Your Skin

If you don't live in a tropical or humid climate, the air in the rooms of your home and/or workplace might be very dry. This affects the eyes, nose, and skin by causing dryness, irritation, and itching. An easy solution is to buy a humidifier. This is totally worth the expense, as it will not only be good for your skin but also for your sinuses and winter-chapped lips. It's even good for your home or office, as it slows down the drying of wooden furniture and prevents cracks in paint and peeling wallpaper (caused, of course, by particularly dry air!). Just be sure to clean it regularly or it can become overrun with bacteria. At the office you can opt for a steam vaporizer, as they are inexpensive and merely boil water into steam; some can be used with aromatic oils. The downside to vaporizers is that they get very hot and need to be on a stable surface away from pets and children.

Remembering Estée Lauder

LORRAINE: What really made Estée Lauder was the glow. Lauder was one of the first skincare companies to create a very light kind of makeup, almost transparent, to enhance the complexion while giving it this very fresh, very healthy luminosity. Estée also oversaw the development of Clinique, created when she recruited Carol Phillips, then the beauty editor at American *Vogue*, along with dermatologist Norman Orentreich, to work on a skincare line focusing on cleansing the skin. This freshness, this cleansing, this glowing complexion was what defined Estée Lauder to me. In that way, she was very French! I still have very vivid memories of her to this day. I once went with Estée to Saks Fifth Avenue in New York, and she used to spritz perfume in the air and walk through the mist of it so that it would land on her hair and clothing and linger deliciously. She had a unique personality.

She often came to Paris in the 1980s, and one time she invited me for lunch at Maxim's. I remember that I didn't touch my lunch (even though it looked exquisite) because I was so mesmerized by her charisma and I was drinking her words.

(See insert for a photo of Estée and Lorraine.)

SPECIAL CARE FOR YOUR EYE AREA

No matter how old you are, an eye contour treatment should become part of your daily routine. The skin under and around your eyes needs extra care because it's thinner and more delicate than the rest of the skin on your face. Compounding this is the fact that there are also fewer sebaceous (oil) glands, so the skin in this area will always be drier, too, and more prone to fine lines and wrinkles. It also has more capillaries leading to your eyes, which often accounts for dark circles or a bluish tint if you are very fair.

In general, fine lines from dehydration are more visible where the skin is the thinnest, which is around the eyes, and also where we tend to have more expression movements due to blinking or squinting. The good news is that when you are thirty, it is easy to get rid of those lines with a rich hydrating cream. After applying a decent amount, the line should totally vanish if it is a dehydration line. When you are thirty-five and up, it becomes a little more difficult to get rid of them because the lines are deeper, so that even when hydrated thoroughly they don't totally disappear.

According to James Kivior, National Education and Events Manager for Eau Thermale Avène, "Taking care of the delicate eye area is very important. The skin around the eye should be treated like the rest of the skin from an early age to help prevent signs of aging. As we get older we need specific ingredients to help encourage cellular turnover, stimulate collagen and hyaluronic acid production, and reduce stagnation under the eyes by increasing circulation. Keep in mind that the concentration of these ingredients should be lower than what is used on the face.

"Once you're in your forties, start to apply a cream. The moisture will increase hydration, and the cream will increase microcirculation, which reduces puffiness."

Another benefit is that when you start using these products regularly, you'll notice that your concealer will go on more smoothly, because your skin will be softer and better hydrated.

Chapter 4

Sun Protection and Travel

Eternity. It's the sea mingled with the sun.
—ARTHUR RIMBAUD

If I close my eyes, I can still remember the wonderful scent of the famous suntan lotion named Huile de Chaldée by Jean Patou that my grandfather would wear on holidays with us. It was made with expensive oils and scented with a warm, sensual mix of flowers "to soften and tan the skin." Its scent became so popular that many customers were buying it purely to inhale its deliciousness. Even my parents would keep a bottle of it at home and use it when they wanted to tan fast.

How crazy is it to think that when I was growing up, tanning (a lot) was still fashionable. How I adored our very own French sun-star, the incomparable Brigitte Bardot, with her love of Saint-Tropez and its gorgeously sunny weather. I used to walk around at home singing one of her famous songs, "Le Soleil"—translated as "Mr. Sun."

Unfortunately, while the sun-worshipping trend is seemingly still in full force every time you go to a popular beach and see hordes of people baking (and burning) all day, consumers now know how important it is to protect themselves from the sun, no matter what their age—because sun exposure is the primary reason skin gets damaged and old before its time. Getting tan-lovers to do it properly, on the other hand, is a work in progress, compounded by the fact that there is no such thing as a "healthy" tan, and sun-induced skin damage is cumulative. You might think you're fine when you're thirty, but by the time you're forty or older, the wrinkles, sun spots, and loss of elasticity will be much more evident.

As world-famous Parisian plastic surgeon Dr. Olivier de Fra-han told me, "Sun is bad, period. Sun is an important cause of bad skin. Along with cigarettes, maybe, and the lack of love!" (Honestly, how French is *that*!)

PROTECTING YOUR FACE (AND BODY) FROM THE SUN

Sun Basics

There are two kinds of UV rays from the sun: UVA (the long waves responsible for aging) and UVB (the short waves responsible for burning, redness, pigmentation, and the superficial damage that occurs immediately after sun exposure). Sunscreen's SPF, or sun protection factor, only measures its protection against UVB rays.

Whatever you do, try to avoid getting burned. The burns you will get from UVB are very harmful, but what's worse is the damage done by UVA at the level of the dermis. UVA rays are very harmful because they cause the most injury to our cells; they are able to reach inside cells and damage the genetic code, impacting the cells' ability to produce good-quality collagen, hyaluronic acid, and the other proteins needed for proper functioning.

In other words, UVA rays from the sun alter your very DNA.

According to Dominique Moyal, Deputy Scientific Director of La Roche-Posay Laboratoire Dermatologique, you need to remember that we need sun protection at all ages—and our skin doesn't become more resistant or adapted to sun exposure over time. It just gets damaged. That is, of course, what a tan is: the visible result of sun damage! Tans and burns over time are one of the direct causes of skin cancer. She suggests that you use a broad-spectrum sunscreen that protects against both UVA and UVB rays and that you use far more than you're likely accustomed to (one tablespoon for your face and one ounce for your body—try measuring it to see how much it actually is!). Also, realize that SPF 50 isn't five times stronger than SPF 10. SPF is a measure of a sunscreen's ability to prevent UVB from damaging the skin and can be used to approximate how many minutes you can remain in the sun without burning. If, for example, you start to burn after twenty minutes, a sunscreen with an SPF of 50 should protect you for 50 times that amount of minutes (approximately 17 hours), but only if you use enough and reapply it constantly.

Another sign of sun damage are brown or white spots. These are called solar lentigines, freckles, liver spots, or just plain old annoying! They are harmless concentrations of pigment, or total lack of pigment with white spots, but you have to be vigilant about them as they will continue to darken or lighten if you do not protect them.

According to James Kivior from Eau Thermale Avène, "The most important thing in treating brown spots is protection from the sun. They can also be lessened with proper products/ingredients. Retinaldehyde, a vitamin-A derivative, helps to encourage cellular renewal, lessening their appearance."

If your spots are dark and well defined, you can ask a dermatologist to remove them. This is usually done with various lasers or liquid nitrogen and is best done during the winter months to limit the effects of UV exposure.

Also, if you have scars, you need extra protection, as you may already have noticed that the skin around a wound is slightly pigmented and not quite the same color as the surrounding area. This is caused by inflammation, which then triggers the pigmentation—the same kind of inflammation produced when your skin gets tanned. Discoloration normally disappears when the wound is fully healed but can become more permanent if exposed to the sun. A high-SPF, broad-spectrum sunscreen is a must.

Sun Exposure Rules

Yes, we all love the sun. It's good for your mood. It energizes and allows the body to synthesize vitamin D, which is essential for many aspects of your health. It also helps with melatonin secretion, which helps regulate your body's natural sleep cycle.

"Some sun exposure on the *body* is beneficial," explains Dr. Philippe Allouche of Biologique Recherche, "but try to avoid sun exposure on the face, as it is constantly under attack by external factors."

So, if you are heading to a sunny destination for your next holiday, follow these rules from pharmacist Claire Bausset about how to be sun-smart. Her *pharmacie* is in the South of France, and she sees so many people walking in every day during the summer, suffering from sunburns that could easily have been prevented.

Rule #1: No sun exposure for children less than three years old.

Rule #2: No sun exposure between one and three p.m. Go outside, especially at the beach, early in the morning or at sunset. In the summer, around five, six, or seven p.m. is a good time to go and relax on the beach.

Rule #3: Use a sunscreen product adapted to your skin sensitivity and renew application every hour and after you swim. Apply it before you leave the house. If you are very pale or at risk for skin cancer, use a long-lasting sunscreen. And remember that sunscreens have a limited life, so you have to buy new products every summer to make sure that you are getting the full protection described on the label.

Rule #4: Many pregnant women develop melasma around the fourth month of their pregnancy. This is caused by the hormonal surge and an increase in melanin synthesis, leading to hyperpigmentation that shows up in the form of dark or grayish spots, often located in the middle of the forehead, on the chin, and around the mouth. Make it a priority to wear a hat, apply a high-SPF sunscreen, and use an anti-pigmentation serum or cream under your sunscreen.

Rule #5: It is essential to hydrate the skin after sun exposure.

Rule #6: If you didn't follow rules 2 and 3, you are likely to get a sunburn. Sunburns are far too common, and they can lead to irreversible damage. It is important to drink a lot of water to rehydrate the skin from within; you can also use a thermal water spray from La Roche-Posay to soothe the burning feeling. A few minutes later, apply a gel that can be used to treat sunburns. (Osmo Soft Gel, available in Europe, works well.) Avoid all exposure to the sun in the following days, and use a sunscreen with maximum protection for the rest of the season. If you have a headache or nausea, aspirin is the best remedy.

In general, wear sun-protective clothing. There are hats, T-shirts, jackets, and rash guards that are made from fabrics that protect against UVA and UVB rays. Look for a UPF (ultraviolet protection factor) label; the higher the number, the greater the protection. These are great options for young children and adults who don't like to use sunscreen.

Prepare and Repair Your Skin Before and After Sun Exposure

New York–based holistic facialist Isabelle Bellis has beautiful skin, and when she talks about sun protection, I always take notes! This is what she recommends:

Before sun exposure, it's always a good idea to prepare your skin with lots of antioxidants to boost the skin's immunity. Eat lots of fresh food containing vitamin C (leafy greens, citrus), vitamin E (oils, almonds, avocado, butternut squash, fish, broccoli), and zinc (nuts, spinach, seafood, pumpkin seeds). A side benefit of eating these nutrients, of course, is that they're great for every aspect of your health.

Avoid any exfoliation or peels fifteen days prior to any extended period of time spent out in the sun, such as a beach vacation. Also stop using products containing any kind of strong acid, such as peels, to prevent damage to the epidermal lipid from oversensitizing your skin.

Avoid skincare products containing alcohol, which can burn the skin, for at least three days.

For sunburn, apply pure aloe vera onto burned areas, but be aware that some products labeled "100 percent pure" still contain alcohol and very little aloe vera. You can even use plain, virgin, sweet almond oil on the burned areas as well. Apply generously to avoid peeling.

It's also very important to cool your skin if it has been burned. Make a compress with fresh chamomile, which is very calming and is a potent anti-inflammatory. The herb holy basil is also very cooling. Herbal cold compresses are easily made: Simply steep tea bags in filtered (very important) hot water and then cool the tea bags in the refrigerator until cold. Soak clean cotton cloth/fabric in chilled tea and squeeze out the excess. Gently apply to burned areas and repeat as necessary.

Our Favorite Sunscreens

For summers in the city, try these tinted SPF products: Erborian CC Crème High Definition Radiance Face Cream Skin Perfector SPF 25 is a multitasking product ideal for women on the run; you put a drop of the Erborian Skin Perfector on and it's white, but when you rub it in, it becomes a tinted moisturizer, and it has a high SPF. For normal to oily skin, try SkinCeuticals Physical Matte UV Defense SPF 50.

I also know how easy it is to get caught up in outdoor activities or to end up sitting on a sunny terrace for lunch. This is when we let our guard down and can unwittingly get a bit too much sun, so use these products that come in convenient small containers and are easy to carry in your purse: Clarins UV PLUS Anti-Pollution Broad Spectrum SPF 50 Tinted Sunscreen, Shiseido UV Protective Liquid Foundation, or Chanel UV Essentiel Multi-Protection Daily Defense Sunscreen Anti-Pollution Broad Spectrum SPF 50.

Anytime you go to the beach, a high-SPF sunscreen is essential. I like Avène, Garnier, La Roche-Posay, Supergoop!, and L'Oréal. And of course a UV T-shirt and a cool hat.

As for Isabelle Bellis, here are her favorites: "I love applying oil, such as the Joëlle Ciocco Elixir Nutritif, underneath sunscreen to create an extra layer of protection. For sunscreen, I highly recommended the MDSolarSciences Mineral Crème SPF 50, which does not clog pores, does not dry out the skin, and does not have a whitening skin effect. As a bonus, this sunscreen is also endorsed by a well-respected cancer research organization."

FOR SPECIAL OCCASIONS, GIVE YOURSELF A GLOW WITH A SELF-TANNER

When I worked for Clarins in London, I was only twenty-one years old, a newbie intern in my first "real job," and I wanted to make a good impression. I especially wanted to get that Clarins glow that everyone in the office seemed to have, yet I was too shy to ask them what products they were using.

When I started going to the office, it was late spring, and all the summer looks were out. Clarins is well known for using beautiful women in their ads—not famous models but women who have that approachable kind of look that makes you wish you were friends with them. As I took the tube to Clarins's offices in Cavendish Place, I had to go up many different, long, *long* escalators that the London Underground is known for. As I went up every day, I passed by the Lancôme ads for their brand-new self-tanners. They might have been the competition, but seeing those ads planted a seed in my head—and I discovered the joys of self-tanning! Luckily, Clarins made a lovely one that worked like a charm, and even though it rained practically every day for the next month, I had my glow and I was very happy.

Use a self-tanner *only* moderately or for special occasions, as it's an easy way to get some color on your skin. Self-tanners used to be tricky, because if you didn't apply them evenly, the streaks would be obvious and there was nothing you could do until they faded away. (And orange palms didn't help!) Everyone's skin reacts slightly differently, so it's worth trying a few brands to find the one that suits you. It's best to start slow and gradually build up color. My secret in the winter, when I have a special occasion coming up and I am very pale, is to mix my self-tanner with a little moisturizer, which gives me some color but not a noticeably fake tan. And if you're planning on going somewhere hot and sunny, you can jump-start your real tan with a self-tanner, applying a small amount first on your face a day or two before you leave, and a bit more the next day if you want more color. You'll arrive at your destination already looking like you've been on the beach—hopefully making you more inclined to spend fewer hours tanning by the pool.

After a few years of experience, I also feel comfortable applying self-tanner on my legs, arms, and décolleté, but if you're not ready, beauty salons or spas have aestheticians who can apply it evenly and you won't have to worry about streaks or blotches.

Fatima Zegrani on How to Apply a Self-Tanner

I met master aesthetician Fatima several years ago in New York when she was working at Clarins. An expert in face and body care, she has also built a reputation for her expertise at applying self-tanners. Here is her method:

Before You Apply

♥ Be careful not to get any manicures, pedicures, or waxing the same day as the treatment. If your skin is normal or oily, purchase a gel or lotion. If your skin is dry, use a creamy formula.

♥ Gels or lotions are easier to apply because they're lighter.

The Day of the Treatment for Your Body

♥ Use a gentle scrub to thoroughly exfoliate your entire body. Wash it off with soap and then rinse well.

♥ Dry yourself thoroughly.

♥ Then apply any body cream or lotion that you like on your feet, knees, hands, and elbows (all the driest areas that sometimes leave marks).

♥ When the cream is completely absorbed, generously apply your self-tanner. Be generous with the application of the product, making sure to apply enough so that it penetrates as you massage.

♥ Cover your entire body, section by section.

♥ For your legs, apply the self-tanner, then massage it in with long strokes. It's like giving yourself a very pleasant massage and is a sure way to get the area fully covered. When you are nearly done and there is a little product left, apply it to your feet.

♥ Finish with a tissue to pat dry the tops of your hands, elbows, knees, and feet area to remove any excess.

The Day of the Treatment for Your Face

♥ Follow the same routine and be sure to use a hydrating cream (in a thin layer) before you apply the self-tanner. I do not recommend using a serum.

♥ Follow with the self-tanner application on your face, avoiding the eyes' contour. At the end of the process, use your fingers to carefully apply around your eyes without getting too close to the eyes themselves.

♥ Finish with a tissue to pat around your hairline and eyebrows.

After the Application

♥ Try not to touch your skin until it is entirely dry. This usually takes about five to ten minutes.

♥ Avoid taking a shower the day you apply a self-tanner. Resume showering the day after.

♥ Make sure to keep your skin hydrated, which allows the tan to stay longer.

And Remember

♥ Always start slow and let the color build up.

♥ Don't ever start a session when you're in a rush—it's very hard to undo an uneven application!

Our Favorite Self-Tanners

Try any of the self-tanners by Caudalie, Clarins, and, for the face, single-use towelettes by Comodynes (which are great for traveling).

LOOKING AFTER YOUR SKIN
WHEN YOU TRAVEL

For All Ages

When I was in my early twenties, I was thrilled to be working for Dior in their Paris office. I was even more thrilled when they told me I needed to go to New York to work on a project with their American team. The day before I was scheduled to leave, a new version of a night cream that was in the process of being developed arrived from the lab. These lab samples always came in simple, white plastic jars with a code on a label—nothing fancy, just the product in development inside.

This particular cream was bright white, with a delicate floral scent. As soon as I tried it, I sighed in pleasure because it smelled so lovely and was instantly super-hydrating. I put one of the little jars in my purse for further testing and applied some of that wonderful cream on my clean face and neck when I was somewhere over the Atlantic. My skin felt better right away, and I also felt protected for the next hours of flight. I know I had a nice glow when I arrived—in part due to my young age, but also due to what was later launched as the Dior Prestige *La Crème de Nuit* (night cream) I was testing.

Ever since that flight, I have always made sure to take extra precautions when I go any distance. I have improved my travel ritual and make sure I cleanse and moisturize my face before a flight, add extra hydration during the flight, and do my own toning facial massage.

I also have a rule to never drink alcohol on the day of the trip and upon arrival. I stick to water and herbal teas to avoid puffiness until after my jet lag is gone.

As the talented journalist and author of books on natural

health Marie-Laure de Clermont-Tonnerre recently wrote in my online magazine:

> Thyme strengthens your immune system. Try drinking a thyme leaf (*Thymus vulgaris*) infusion when you wake up. It is very efficient in fighting infections, and it also provides a necessary boost in the morning. Lemon is also very good. It cleans your liver, and freshens your complexion.
>
> To prepare your decoction of lemons, bring one quart of water to a boil with a full organic lemon (rind included since the rind is where the essential oils reside) for ten minutes along with two sticks of cinnamon (or half a teaspoon of ground cinnamon). Mash the lemon with a fork in the water, strain, and drink as hot as possible. Cinnamon is an excellent tonic, with antibacterial and antiviral properties that protect you from infections.

And using a simple saline nasal spray is also an absolute must. I use it every day, but when I travel I usually keep it in my bag so I don't forget to hydrate and clean my nose.

As for my mother, she always tells me, "On my travel day, I apply makeup only on my eyes and keep my face clean so that I can add more moisturizer or a facial oil to my skin."

My In-Flight Beauty Kit

I keep sample or travel sizes in my travel bag and replenish them after a trip, so I am always good to go! These are my must-haves:

- ♥ Hand sanitizer (Burt's Bees, Purell, Byredo Rinse-free hand wash)

- ♥ Hydrating hand cream (Aerin, Clarins) and a nail file
- ♥ Lip balm (Bioderma, Homeoplasmine) and a lip gloss
- ♥ Herbal teas (Kusmi Tea Detox or Pukka Detox or Cleanse)
- ♥ Snacks (almonds, 85 percent dark chocolate as a replacement for a heavy dessert)
- ♥ Earplugs, sleep mask
- ♥ Travel-size facial moisturizer (Nuxe, Pai)
- ♥ A concealer and a very light foundation to apply before landing, such as the easy-to-carry Dior Capture Totale Dreamskin Perfect Skin Cushion, perfect for on-the-go touch-ups
- ♥ A pair of compression stockings is a must for any flights over three hours. They really make a tremendous difference in improving your circulation and lessening travel bloat. (For more on this topic, see page 147 in Chapter 7.)

The Best Travel Tips from French Beauty Experts

Prisca Courtin-Clarins's Beauty Travel Kit for the Plane

Plane travel dehydrates the skin a lot. I recommend drinking a lot of water during the flight and hydrating the skin with Clarins Hydra-Essentiel. Also, use Clarins Moisture Replenishing Lip Balm with essential rose wax. Clarins Energizing Emulsion is *the* miracle product to keep your legs from swelling.

As for my daily beauty routine when I travel, I want to keep it as thorough as it is at home, so I pack whatever I use daily but in travel size. (All my products are by Clarins!) For the face, I use Double Serum, Multi-Active Day Cream SPF 20, Toning Lotion with Chamomile,

Instant Eye Make-Up Remover, and Gentle Foaming Cleanser with Cottonseed. For the body, the Tonic Body Balm and Tonic Body Treatment Oil are my favorites. I tend to use pretty natural makeup: Supra Volume black mascara (which also stimulates lash growth), Clarins BB Skin Perfecting SPF, and Clarins Blush Prodige Illuminating Cheek Colour Sweet Rose. I also use the line Leonor Greyl Shampooing Reviviscence for my hair.

Claire Bausset's Beauty Travel Kit

- Konjac sponge, which has a double use: cleansing and soft makeup removal in one
- René Furterer Solaire Nourishing Repair Shampoo, which repairs hair from the drying effects of UV rays, salt, and chlorine
- Bioderma Hydrabio Moisturizing Anti-UV Mist SPF 30
- Bioderma Hydrabio Crème

Isabelle Bellis's Beauty Travel Kit and Best Travel Tips

- Avène SpringThermal Water Spray
- Joëlle Ciocco Lait Onctueux Capital
- Joëlle Ciocco Lotion Lactée
- Joëlle Ciocco Elixir Nutritif
- Lavender essential oil
- A beautiful hat and a long-sleeved surfing T-shirt

According to Isabelle Bellis, you should make these adjustments to your skincare routine when traveling:

- At least a week before flying, you should avoid any strong treatments/procedures, which can aggravate your skin during travel. Plus, the airplane cabin is not completely sanitary, so it's best to have your skin's immunity strong and healthy to protect against this challenging environment.

▼ An airplane cabin can be very drying. When flying, I strongly recommend traveling with bare skin, without any makeup, which can be even more drying while flying and prevent the skin from breathing properly.

▼ It's also important to prepare your skin before traveling by air. Cleanse your face thoroughly with a gentle cleanser and then apply a rich base—like an oil. (Avoid commercially available towelettes, which are very practical but full of drying chemicals.) Apply a moisturizer to create a protective seal/barrier to keep moisture in. A moisturizer with a heavier consistency is best to prevent water evaporation. Avoid retinol-based creams, which can exacerbate dehydration.

▼ A big mistake many air travelers make is to spray/mist water on their faces. As water attracts water, spraying/misting water will dry out the skin even more. Drink water but do not *apply* water.

▼ Don't forget to moisturize your hands, which can get dry as well. Also, keep your hands off your face as much as you can.

▼ Apply makeup right before you arrive/land and never before or during the middle of your flight. You might feel a bit less glamorous during your flight, but I assure you that you will look more glamorous when you exit the plane!

▼ Postflight, a nourishing mask, followed by a good moisturizer, can be very beneficial.

Chapter 5

Maintaining Your Youthful Skin Without the Doctor (and Sometimes With!)

What is beauty? An idea, a feeling, a pleasure, an emotion. And yet a mystery at the same time. Beauty, like time, is something no one truly understands. No definition can ever fully capture beauty.

—JEAN D'ORMESSON, *GUIDE DES ÉGARÉS*

*M*any of the specialists in this chapter are highly skilled beauty experts who use techniques that do not require invasive treatments. They do not have a medical approach, yet they leave their clients with remarkable results in terms of radiance, youth, and a demonstrable improvement in their skin. The glow is worth so much, so read on—and see how you can use their advice for your own treatments at home.

One wonderful bit of advice comes from L'Oréal's Elisabeth Bouhadana: "You must always remember that it is easier to protect than to correct. That is something that, psychologically, women do not like to hear. It explains why Botox and other instant treatments work so well. But even Botox, in the long term, isn't as effective; the dosage must be increased, it can alter your features, and the effect will never be as stunning as it was the first time. Same goes for the different types of injections, such as fillers. An injection of hyaluronic acid works right away to firm up the cheeks and helps make the wrinkles disappear. It gives a lifting effect, but it doesn't last. Especially if you do it too often—it creates pockets that have a tendency to deflate . . . and then you need more injections. That's why you can see older women with their cheeks unnaturally high. And the day they stop the injections, they look much older because gravity takes over."

YOU DON'T NEED THE NEEDLE WHEN AN *INSTITUT DE BEAUTÉ* IS JUST AROUND THE CORNER

French women have a lifelong love affair with their local *institut de beauté,* or beauty salon, as I mentioned in Chapter 1. Some of my favorite memories from growing up are when I went to the Adrienne Institut de Beauté, rue Vignon, near the Place de la Madeleine. It was run by two sisters, Colette and Jocelyne, and their little booths where you got your treatments were side by side. It was located at the back of a lovely courtyard—very Parisian-style, where most of the buildings have large outer doors that open to courtyards within. It was very quiet, with the large, heavy entrance doors blocking out noise from the streets. It made you feel far away from the hustle and bustle of the city and its traffic. The *institut* was very feminine with its elegant choice of pale pink and white for the decor. My mother went all the time, and she took me for the first time for my own treatment when I was fourteen. I can still remember my very first waxing there, the smell of that thick, deep pink wax, and how nice it was to have my legs so smooth after. Whenever I went with my mother, we would chat about what had happened at work that day and about beauty techniques while we got our eyelashes tinted. The two sisters would recommend the latest sun-care products. I felt so grown up!

What I learned at this *institut de beauté* wasn't just about how to take care of my skin. I realized that something magical can happen when you have an expert take care of you. Not only do you look better, but you feel so much more confident.

What's more, I was taught that seeing these experts was simply another part of my routine. They totally normalized the need to ask for beauty help and tips. The word often used is *pampering*, but that implies luxury and a high price tag. Our local *institut* was not expensive. I would much rather have gone without a new pair of shoes than give up those visits that made me look so great and feel so wonderful.

My grandmother and mother also loved their salons—and it showed!

RÉGINE: Paris had a few wonderful beauty salons in the 1950s. All the chic Parisian women would go to the Elizabeth Arden salon on the Place Vendôme; it's where I went to get my hair done. Artists and actresses would flock to Helena Rubinstein or Max Factor, located in all the chicest neighborhoods of Paris. Revlon's salon was mostly for manicures. These American brands were seen as just as chic and high quality as the French salons, rivaling their luxurious décor, the beautiful brocade sofas and the thick carpets that muffled the outside noise, and the quality of their aestheticians.

Some Parisian women stayed faithful to the French brands, such as Françoise Morice or Guerlain. As soon as you walked in the door of the Guerlain salon, you would be enveloped by the wonderful scent of Shalimar. This was one of the first salons to offer skincare treatments, like facials. For many women, the Guerlain salon was a way to touch luxury. The Champs-Elysées is no longer what it used to be, but in the 1950s it was one of the best locations in Paris, with classically elegant décor and a grandeur to attract the wealthy women who would arrive in their chauffeur-driven Rolls-Royces, wearing fur coats and holding onto their crocodile bags by the Maison Germaine Guerin. Up until the 1980s, many Parisian women lived and dressed in a much more glamorous way—*Un Luxe Apparent*. It is very different now with a much more casual esthetic in the salons that cater to this same demographic.

FACIAL MASSAGE IS THE FRENCH WOMAN'S BEST-KEPT SECRET

My friends in New York always ask me what it is that French women do to have such wonderful skin, and I tell them that one of our best-kept secrets is the face massage. This is without doubt the single best noninvasive treatment you can do to improve the quality of your facial skin.

My grandmother used to go to Elizabeth Arden for her facial massages. My mother would go to Ingrid Millet, who also took care of former First Lady Madame Claude Pompidou and the actress Isabelle Adjani. Chic Parisiennes, in fact, jealously guard the names of their favorite facial massage aestheticians from even their most trusted friends!

In France, facial massage is a way of life. Fortunately, you can now find salons and spas all over the world where aestheticians have been trained in these techniques. Not only have I found a few across the Atlantic already, but one experience was particularly memorable. As usual, my antenna was out in hopes of capturing any good beauty advice when I heard a friend of a friend start talking about a wonderful facialist. I got the aesthetician's name (thankfully, Americans are not so secretive about their skincare professionals!) and made an appointment. The woman who greeted me was so lovely, and I really liked her from the moment I met her. While she was doing my face massage, we were happily chatting about French beauty salons, as she used to be the right hand of the famous Ingrid Millet. So I said to her, "You must have known my mother when she was *Vogue*'s beauty editor."

She stopped, smiled, and asked, "Are you Lorraine's daughter?"

I laughed and told her yes. The rest you can now imagine—not only do I continue to see her regularly, but we always have so much to share from her years in France, especially as she knew my mother and they had so much fun in Paris during those years.

Facial massages tone and hydrate the skin and give you a great glow. Just as working out tightens the muscles of your body, facial massage tightens your skin. Regularly practicing these methods of molding stimulates the muscles of the face in areas that usually hollow with age.

French women love facial massages for a whole variety of reasons. First, they stimulate circulation, which awakens the complexion. Massages don't hurt; they actually make you feel wonderful. Massages are also completely manual, making them eco-conscious, and they don't need any special (or expensive) equipment. Results are guaranteed if you do it regularly and properly; and, of course, they are a beloved and well-kept secret! No wonder that the best facial-massage specialists in Paris are frequented by well-known French celebrities. They know that you'll look as if you had a mini natural face-lift, and you'll need a lot less makeup because your skin will look so good.

I'll show you how to do this at home on the following page.

Nicole Desnoë, Founder of the Nicole Desnoë Face Massage Technique, on Why Facial Massage Is so Effective

Nicole Desnoë is one of the most famous facialists in Paris and has been giving her unique facial massages to women for over fifty years. One of the most potent steps in her treatment is the *pincement Jacquet*, which is difficult to translate but basically means a light pinch around the oval of the face, always with the motions moving upward toward the crown of the head and around the lines at each side of your mouth. Nicole's expert hands will massage between the eyebrows, above the lips, and on the front and the back of the neck.

Nicole's technique is distinctive because it creates an anti-aging effect by massaging the skin, not pulling it. "The massage puts into action a whole circulation system and stimulates the production of collagen. If your muscles are contracted, you can't be beautiful; massages are what de-contracts these parts of the body," she explains. "The muscles of the face are linked to the bone structure. To develop the muscles of your body, you need to exercise; to develop the face muscles, you need a *deep* massage, which is totally different than a superficial one. It prevents the skin from sagging so that muscles retain their elasticity and remain firm. It's the only kind of massage that's therapeutic, because it's deep, energizing, and has fast results. It reaches below the surface. I'm convinced that without massages you can't obtain positive results. You can use all the anti-wrinkle creams that you want, but they won't work as well without massages. In other words, hydration is important, but it's not used for firming, and it can never stimulate the muscles of your face.

"Women in their forties look for an anti-wrinkle regimen. And that starts with massaging, the first and main anti-wrinkle treatment. For women over fifty, when they come and they say, 'Nicole, what should I do?' I tell them that I will do my massages more frequently than I would for younger women to get rid of the wrinkles they have already. It doesn't mean that they will be completely wrinkle-free, but it will stop it from getting worse.

"Most importantly, above all else, is good hygiene, which means healthy eating, good sleeping patterns, time for rest, and hygiene of the self. And, of course, nourishing through massage; because if you don't massage, it doesn't work."

I EASILY LEARNED TO DO MY OWN FACIAL

Isabelle Bellis, like Nicole, is a staunch advocate of manual facial massage. Although there are other advanced treatments that utilize technology, electricity, and machines to bring the skin back to life, she considers it the most effective, efficient, and safe method to achieve natural, balanced, and healthy skin.

If you can't book an appointment with a facialist, do not despair. A very easy way to create a few special moments in your beauty routine is to add a few minutes of facial massage.

Sometimes I do this on weekends, as I can more easily carve out a few minutes for myself in the morning; otherwise, I do it in the evening after cleansing my face. Whether in my bathroom or in bed—if I'm watching a little TV to unwind before bedtime, for example—I try to do my massages regularly to get good results.

Choose one of your moisturizers that has a smooth texture, as this will facilitate the massage and allow your fingers to slide easily. Avoid any creams that have a sticky texture or that could start to peel while you massage. Usually a hazelnut-size amount of a cream or oil is enough for the face, and another one should be used for the neck and décolleté.

The French Facial Massage

1. Massage the Eye Area

You need a very small amount of cream to massage the eye contour. Place a dot of cream on the tip of your index or middle finger and pat it under both eyes. Apply a light pressure along the bone of your eye socket. For more mature skin, use one index finger to hold skin taut while the other finger applies the eye cream.

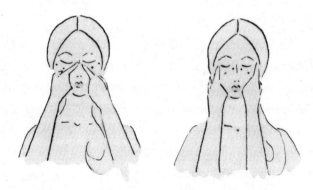

Alternatively, place the tips of your fingers under your eyes and apply light pressure as you move up toward the outer corners of your eyes. Then repeat this motion from the bridge of your nose along the brows to the outer corners of your eyes.

Next, pinch along your brows toward your temples.

2. Massage the Frown Lines, Between Your Eyes

Use both index fingers to create a knitting-like motion or zig-zag between your brows. You can do that for two or three minutes a day.

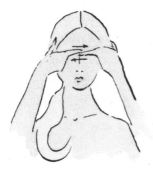 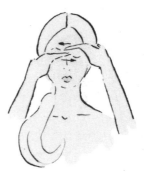

3. Massage the Lips

Use the same small amount of cream as you did for the eye massage. With two fingers, hold the left side of your upper lip taut while your right finger glides above the upper lip. Repeat this exercise on the other side of the mouth.

Complete the massage beneath the lower lip. This will help prevent the little wrinkles above the lip.

4. Drainage (helps to remove fluid and congestion from your skin)

Place your thumbs under your chin, then use your index fingers as pliers as you pinch along your jawline up to your ears. Repeat five times.

5. Massage Your Neck and Décolleté

Lightly pinch the skin beneath your chin where the neck meets the jaw. Practice an upward movement toward the ears for a lifting effect.

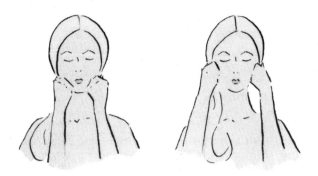

Place your hand flat on your neck beneath your ear, parallel to the jawline. Then, slide your hand firmly down toward your chest/décolleté. Keep your fingers together, thumb included, to avoid touching the thyroid.

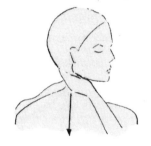
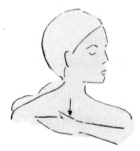

FRENCH WOMEN ALSO LOVE THEIR FACIALS

Just as a facial massage is one of a French woman's best-kept secrets, so is her facialist. Women in some other countries don't see facials the way we do. For them, facials are touted as not much more than a lovely pampering hour where your face is examined, hydrated, and a few zits squeezed out—a nice indulgence once in a while but certainly not a necessity.

For us, on the other hand, a facial is a must-have step in our skin-protection arsenal. We know that good facials not only keep our skin in top shape but have a cumulative effect, especially over the years. They can add firmness, even out blotchy skin tone, reduce pigmentation spots, treat acne, plump up dry skin, and even reduce the appearance of fine lines. Your aesthetician will discuss your skincare concerns and treat them specifically. Be sure to shop around for someone you like, who listens to you, and whose treatments are effective and affordable. A good facialist is worth her weight in gold! The more you do it, and the earlier you start, the better you'll look. And one of the reasons, which you have likely figured out by now, is due to the potent effect of the massage element during the treatment.

For *jeunesse,* I would recommend a facial once every three months or so. For *plénitude,* once every two months. For *maturité,* once a month, if possible. You should start to see results within a few weeks of getting regular facials.

WISE CHOICES ON YOUR PLATE
WILL SHOW ON YOUR FACE

Beautiful, healthy skin isn't just dependent on your skincare products and facial massages. Eating skin-friendly foods will improve your complexion as well. For the past two years, my brother and sister have paid more attention to the freshness and quality of their food, cut down on gluten and dairy, and put more emphasis on plant-based rather than animal-based proteins; doing so made visible changes to their appearance. Not only is their skin clearer and less tired-looking, but even the whites of their eyes appear whiter and their hair is thicker and more lustrous.

These tips have been compiled thanks to what I learned from Dr. Georges Mouton, internationally renowned expert in functional medicine; Isabelle Bellis; Nicole Desnoë; and Biologique Recherche's Dr. Phillipe Allouche:

- Many people suffer from dry skin because they lack healthy fat in their diet. Healthy fats are found in plant sources such as olive oil and avocado, which are full of omega-9 fatty acids; in almonds, which contain omega-6 fatty acids; and in other nuts, fish, and chia seeds, which contain omega-3 fatty acids. A side benefit is that these fats lubricate your internal tissues and are vital to healthy hormone function. Musts to avoid are trans fats and any fats that are solid at room temperature.

- It's a good idea to reduce caffeinated beverages, which are very diuretic and create more dryness.

- Fish oil is also an excellent source of vitamin A, a natural retinol, which nourishes your entire system.

- Drinking wine at dinner is fine, especially red wine that is loaded with antioxidants, but more than one small glass isn't recommended.

- Citrus fruits are excellent for the complexion. Cucumbers are packed with vitamins, nutrients, and antioxidants. Zucchini have a high water content and are packed with nutrients, as long as you don't peel them. Tomatoes are loaded with vitamins A and K, while parsley and kiwi are full of vitamin C.

- Try to avoid eating very spicy food.

- Make sure your food is diverse and colorful.

Our Favorite Advanced Treatment Is Microcurrent Therapy

My grandmother, my mother, and I swear by this treatment. Because it has worked so well for us, I am including it so you can consider whether or not it might work for you.

Microcurrent therapy uses an electrical current that flows through the skin and facial muscles, causing them to tighten. It feels like an hour of facial massaging. Usually, the aesthetician first slathers on a conducting gel and then works two wands with opposite currents over your face. It is not at all painful; on the contrary, you may end up drifting off into a very pleasant semi-dream state. Afterward, your face will look rested and full . . . and youthful!

According to skincare expert Philippe Simonin, "Electrical stimulation of the skin brings outstanding results and fights effectively against signs of aging like wrinkles and loss of elasticity. Like facial massage, it helps to enhance your natural collagen and elastin levels by improving circulation and reeducating the underlying facial muscles. It's like a great workout for your face—and the more you do it, the more toned your skin will be."

Carmel O'Neill is the expert of microcurrent treatments in New York City, where she runs the Renew Anti-Aging Center. I see her once a month for treatment and learned the following:

Microcurrent is among the most effective noninvasive anti-aging technology treatments available. It works with your own body's electrical current to tone and lift the neck, jaw, and eye area. It reduces and eliminates fine lines and wrinkles; increases cellular activity; increases collagen and elastin levels; improves sun damage, rosacea, acne, and melasma; stimulates your circulation to reduce inflammation and dark circles; and improves hydration and receptivity to nutrients. It has immediate, visible results.

As a quick starter, treatments should be performed once or twice a week for best results, and can then be reduced to maintenance treatment every one to three months.

If you don't want to go to a salon for this treatment, you can do what my mother does and use what she calls a little miracle of a device, the Nu Skin Facial Spa, two or three times a week. Its at-home microcurrent treatment will give you just the glow you're seeking.

IF YOU DO GET DERMATOLOGICAL TREATMENTS

As noninvasive procedures like Botox, injectable fillers, chemical peels, and lasers become more and more popular, it's important for you to treat your skin with great care after you have anything done. Even if you have all your treatments done solely by a licensed dermatologist or plastic surgeon who gives trusted advice, remember that strong treatments can weaken your skin— with laser treatments and peels, new skin layers are exposed to the elements and are particularly susceptible to sun damage—so it's tremendously important to follow up with products and techniques that help rebuild your skin, keep it well hydrated and replenished, and allow it to heal. The last thing you want to do is use any skincare products containing ingredients that can cause further irritation.

Avène is one of the best-known French brands of thermal water sprays and other skincare products (available in American drugstores, too!). My mother, grandmother, and I have used it to refresh our skin for as long as I can remember. According to James Kivior, National Education and Events Manager at Avène, two of their products, Avène Thermal Spring Water and Cicalfate Restorative Skin Cream, are used by doctors and aestheticians after laser resurfacing and chemical peels. They've been specifically designed to reduce inflammation while helping to repair and protect compromised skin. This also makes them ideal in case you've gotten sunburned. The Thermal Spring Water contains a low mineral content that will soothe and soften the skin, and it has a neutral pH that will not disrupt the skin's natural pH, which is compromised during peels and laser treatments. It also contains unique microflora, giving it its anti-inflammatory and anti-pruritic properties.

For postoperative care, you might want to try the Avène line for intolerant skin, which contains minimal ingredients, can help reduce future reactivity, and is soothing and reparative.

THE APPOINTMENT MOST FRENCH WOMEN WILL NEVER ADMIT THEY MADE . . . WITH A PLASTIC SURGEON

RÉGINE: In the 1950s, plastic surgery was not common, but for those who did want a little work, the most-requested procedure was a nose job. Only much later did women start to do other things. The famous surgeon in those days was Charles Claoué, and he was so popular that we would say of some women, "Oh, she has the Claoué nose!"

LORRAINE: In the 1960s, we started to do more procedures, but French women will mostly go to a surgeon for small work, little by little. In general, they are wary of having one big lift. A French woman does not want people to see what she is doing; she is very discreet. She does not want her face to change too much or to have that shiny plastic lookalike look.

So why am I including a section on plastic surgery in a chapter telling you that you don't need the needle or the scalpel to look your best? Because, according to Dr. Olivier de Frahan, the most renowned plastic surgeon in Paris, some procedures are designed for certain skincare issues that simply can't be treated by anything other than more intense treatments—but only as a last resort. The more informed you are about these procedures, the more you can decide whether or not a little work might be right for you—now, sometime in the future, or never. Dr. de Frahan is not the kind of practitioner who will take on just any patient, and his attitude should inform anyone considering plastic surgery, regardless of age.

As he explains:

Women start coming to see me, unfortunately, when they are around eighteen or twenty years old. They are much younger these days than they used to be. In fact, for the younger generation, the first language in the world is the language of images. The younger generation is overloaded with images. Most of the time these images are retouched, fake, but since these people are constantly taking photos

of themselves, they compare themselves to these images and therefore become totally insecure. They want to conform to models and
are totally unforgiving toward themselves. A playground for fourteen-
year-olds is a nightmare of abuse and judgment these days. There is
a kind of tribe phenomenon; they join a 'tribe,' which they can identify with, dress alike, apply makeup the same way, adopt the same
hairstyle, and it's a terrible thing. Rather than embracing diversity,
they all want to look alike. It's very difficult for these young people
(teenagers mostly) to be different, to have a different kind of beauty
or a different personality. I think that the French school system doesn't
encourage differences. Its goal is to fit the greatest number into the
same mold.

What I have learned from this illuminating meeting with
Dr. de Frahan is that when girls are eighteen or twenty, they follow in their mothers' footsteps. If their mothers went in for regular Botox injections, they'll ask for it as well, as they have already
seen the results.

Dr. de Frahan noticed this deep insecurity, and more often
than not he has to say no—to the point that in an article published about him, the headline was DOCTOR NO. Sometimes, he
explained, he'll see lovely older women who do not think they
are pretty—because they think they don't look pretty in the eyes
of the man they are with, or because they are not well adjusted or
happy. His sharp eye could ascertain those kinds of potential
patients, and he would decline to help them. Being the expert, he
can say, "You are very beautiful," and know they will listen.

"I think that French women are different than women from
other cultures in that they are more natural, less perfectionist,
more pragmatic. They have a better relationship with their image,

their kind of beauty. I have a big New York clientele, and it is very different. They want perfection. It is a challenge; it is a competition. To be a woman means entering a competition, and everything has to be perfect. I also started seeing a lot of injection overdoses looking for repair. They have been injected so many times that their cheekbones look like balloons. I call it the lunchtime lifting—they go with their girlfriends at lunchtime to get injections. When it reaches the level of overdose, it doesn't go away. It stays that way. I can spot it in three seconds and from ten meters away because there is nothing natural about it. Often, it is impossible to fix."

Now he has a second wave of patients, mostly from New York and Los Angeles, who have seen the damage that can be done with an overdose of injections, but still do not want to look old. They've done their research and are well informed about their requests. They still want to look like themselves, so they want a discreet type of surgery, mostly for the eyelids. "They want a natural result so they will be able to lie and say that they had nothing done!" he adds with a laugh.

Postsurgery, he is always amazed to see how fast the body recovers, and one of his recommendations is for lymphatic drainage. This gentle pressure technique is used to move fluids that might have built up. It helps with the recovery process and to restore the skin's elasticity. You should also use an over-the-counter scar-reducing cream to help the healing and to mask the scar until it fades away, and use Vaseline to keep the skin hydrated.

As beauty editors, our view when it comes to plastic surgery is the less visible, the better. The best way is to proceed with small touches: contouring the face, lightening the eye by correcting the eyelids, adding hyaluronic acid if necessary to erase certain deep wrinkles. These little touch-ups have the advantage of refreshing and rejuvenating, unlike a total face lift, which can sometimes freeze the face and remove all the expressions that make up the life and personality of a woman.

Chapter 6

Beautiful Makeup at Any Age

*The most beautiful makeup for a woman
is passion. But cosmetics are easier to buy.*

—YVES SAINT LAURENT

Doing your makeup the French way is the result of experience, good products, a perfectly clean face, a less-is-more philosophy . . . and tips from experts.

My grandmother was entirely self-taught. She had to be, because when she started modeling at the end of the 1940s, there were no makeup artists or hairdressers on sets. She practiced at home by copying the looks of the most glamorous and beautiful Hollywood stars—Joan Crawford for her lips; Marlene Dietrich for her ultrathin eyebrows, and then Audrey Hepburn for her thick ones; Ava Gardner for everything because she was so astonishingly gorgeous.

It is also interesting to think about how many changes makeup trends have gone through over the decades—not just color choices but technology. In the 1950s, for example, French women wore their hats and gloves every day; they not only looked chic and well put-together, but sunscreen was not yet available, and this helped protect their faces and hands from the sun—as did the heavier pancake foundation that was popular at the time. Now, of course, few women wear hats and gloves every day (although I wish they would!), and foundation formulas are so much lighter yet give the same coverage without clogging pores. But the love for an indelibly red lip has stayed the same.

MAKEUP TIPS FOR ALL AGES

Jeunesse and *Plénitude*:

My typical work or casual/daytime makeup routine is very simple, and it is youthful yet sophisticated.

- On a perfectly clean and hydrated face and neck, I start by covering my dark circles with a Laura Mercier Secret Camouflage compact, or I use a thin drop of It Cosmetics concealer Bye Bye Under Eye, a densely pigmented texture that covers all imperfections. Like my mother, I love YSL Touche Éclat, and I dab a little bit on top—it's not only a concealer but a light reflector that makes your skin come alive.
- Next, I apply a tinted BB cream or foundation. So many brands now have exquisite textures that let your skin breathe and look very natural. Some of my favorite BB or all-in-one creams are Erborian or Dior Capture Totale Dreamskin Advanced; my favorite foundations are By Terry, Edward Bess, or Georgio Armani Beauty.

If I choose a foundation instead of a BB or CC cream, I usually mix and match products that give me the best results. While it works for some women to build the perfect complexion with layers, I am more a "mixer" of textures and colors. Mixing two foundations together, I get the perfect color for my skin tone. Sometimes I even add a complexion enhancer, such as the Estée Lauder Revitalizing Supreme+ Global Anti-Aging Wake Up Balm, Charlotte Tilbury Wonderglow, or the Sisley Paris Instant Éclat. Their sheen will add that little plus for a very radiant and natural result.

- If I'm going to be in the sun during a workday, I'll use a foundation with SPF protection by either SkinCeuticals, Erborian, or Supergoop!
- To enhance my cheekbones, I add a touch of bronzer and blush by either Guerlain, Clarins, Charlotte Tilbury, Clinique, or my mother's standby, Bobbi Brown.
- The last touch is dark mascara by YSL or Chanel and occasionally a light pink lipstick or gloss from either Clarins, Tata Harper, Sisley Paris, or Clé de Peau.

For nights out, I use a bit more of everything:

- I start by using either a serum or a light moisturizer.
- Next, I apply a primer, usually either by Guerlain or By Terry, followed by a foundation.
- I like to use a little powder, but I avoid the darker ones and highlight my cheeks with tones of pink or peach.
- For my lips, I have learned to "crayon" them on—I outline my lips with a neutral lip liner and delicately fill them in. (A trick I learned from my grandmother!) Then

I apply my lipstick. This will make your lipstick last for hours.

♥ I usually still have the mascara on from earlier that day, so I just need to make my eyes more *travaillés*— polished—with some black crayon liner and dark gray shades of eye shadow.

♥ On weekends with my husband, I'll still wear a little mascara and create a natural glow on my skin with a light foundation and just a touch of powder. It's feminine without looking overdone. These days, I like Capture Totale Dreamskin Cushion by Dior. It's the perfect go-to product for a fresher and more radiant complexion.

French Makeup Favorites

I follow the advice from expert French makeup artist Muriel Baurens: "You need to have a *light hand* when applying your makeup. And the older you are, the lighter it needs to get."

These are the favorite choices of several of my Parisian friends:

For the Face:

♥ Laura Mercier Secret Camouflage (a two-shade compact to conceal dark circles)

♥ Nars Radiant Creamy Concealer (has a luxurious texture and multiple shades)

♥ Clarins Instant Smooth Perfecting Touch (fills in the appearance of fine lines)

♥ Fluid Sheer by Giorgio Armani (works as a liquid highlighter)

♥ Guerlain Météorites Baby Glow (gives a very natural glow to the complexion)

- By Terry Glow-Expert Duo Stick
- Guerlain face powders
- Nars The Multiple Stick

For the Eyes:
- Lancôme Grandiôse mascara
- Marc Jacobs Beauty Highliner Gel Eye Crayon (waterproof)
- Eye shadows by Chanel, Lancôme, and Sisley Paris

For the Eyebrows:
- Benefit Gimme Brow Volumizing Eyebrow Gel
- Glossier Boy Brow (works as a brow filler and shaper)

For the Lips:
- Sisley Paris Phyto-Lip Twist
- Chanel lipsticks
- Clinique Chubby Sticks
- For matte lips: By Terry Rouge-Expert Click Stick

MY MOTHER'S MAKEUP ROUTINE

Plénitude and *Maturité*

LORRAINE: When I was a little girl, on the way back from elementary school, my grandmother would pick me up because my mother was at work. Once a week, we'd always stop at a small *parfumerie* on the rue de la Tour for a special visit. This was a little gem of a shop where the owner mixed up her own moisturizers and would recommend the latest products. On a very lucky day, I would be able to watch as she'd hand-blend different-colored powders, taking bits from enormous jars that held purple, green, and yellow powder made by T. LeClerc and then cut them together until she had created the perfect tone for my grandmother's skin. Then she'd gently place the powder in a round container and top it off with a huge puff. It was like watching a magician at work!

In 1969, I was nineteen years old and got a job for a short time at American *Vogue* as assistant to Susan Train, who was then the fashion editor and Parisian correspondent for the magazine. Veruschka was the top model and was often photographed on location by Franco Rubartelli. Veruschka used to do her own makeup on these shoots—even if they were in the deep jungle—and she was so proficient that she could make herself look like a panther or a tiger or any other kind of exotic creature.

One day, there was a photo shoot at the country house of the artists François-Xavier and Claude Lalanne in Ury. Their studio was there, too. They had designed a snake on a tapestry, and Franco had placed it on a white cliff so Veruschka could pose next to it. Franco used to photograph me as well, and he told me something I always remembered: "Don't ever touch the shape of your eyebrows; it is what gives you your personality and defines who you are."

I was fascinated by how Veruschka so easily did her makeup—I can still so clearly see her with her brushes and her jars of white powder from Eve of Roma, which she loved to use around her eyes to illuminate and enhance them. Watching her do her makeup so effortlessly is actually what triggered my love for beauty and makeup. It's why I decided to work in that field.

This choice was reinforced when I first met Diana Vreeland in Paris. She was staying, as mentioned earlier in the book, at the elegant Hôtel de Crillon in a suite overlooking the Place de la Concorde. Although it was still early in the morning, she was already made up for the day with her signature crimson lipstick, her shiny and sleek black hair pulled back into a bun, and her long fingernails painted. After that meeting, Diana invited me to come to New York so she could introduce me to the beauty brands that were finding success there, so that I could work for one of them.

I was mesmerized on this first visit to New York to see the beauty counters at the department stores—it was a bit of a shock, with so much merchandise for sale, and then to encounter the salespeople, who took a very different approach from the neighborhood *pharmacies* and *parfumeries* I had grown up with. I still remember discovering the brand Kiehl's, as it was one of the first apothecary-type family beauty businesses to become so successful in America.

My makeup routine has basically remained the same for the last forty years. The only real difference is the use of new products with wonderful textures that improve skin radiance and brighten the complexion. I love trying new things. In the mid-sixties, Revlon had a wonderful powder-blush called Blush-On that one could apply with a small makeup brush. It allowed for a very light application. Then Clinique launched its famous lip gloss called First in Color in the early 1970s. It was a small box with a lip cream. Max Factor also launched its Pure Magic Lip Gloss. It came in individual little jars that were very desirable, which all the journalists at French *Vogue* loved. Yves Saint Laurent had an extravagant fuchsia color; Estée Lauder had its Éclat Doré tint; and Revlon the Face Gleamer, a blush stick that was totally revolutionary and gave you the glow. Everyone was trying the new face powders with opalescent, iridescent, and pearlescent pigments—they all wanted to have either tanned skin or gleaming iridescent skin. Even our lips were shiny with gloss. Maybe it was the influence of disco, but in the seventies, beauty had a distinctive and dazzling radiance.

This is my makeup routine now:

♥ I use a toner or a spritz of thermal water and then my face cream as a base for my makeup. I use moisturizing creams with different textures depending on the season; in the winter, I favor a thicker texture and in the spring or the summer, I use a lighter and more fluid one. My mother shared the tip she'd learned from the Carita sisters (founders of the famous Carita Beauty Salon in Paris) about avoiding heavy or oil-based creams if I want my makeup to last for a long time, so I followed her advice about what serum to use before I put my makeup on.

♥ These days I am trying a fabulous new cream from SkinCeuticals. Instead of concealer, I use YSL Touche Éclat around my eyes, which is one of the best inventions ever in beauty products. I have it in its various shades. On top I add a bit of white powder applied with a small brush to freshen up the eye contour.

♥ For eye color, first I apply a neutral, nude base on my eyelids, either By Terry or YSL Couture Eye Primer, and then add a light neutral color on top. I apply black eyeliner, and I play with the shadows as Christine from Carita taught me. I am always looking for the best dark black eye crayon with a texture that does not smudge. I can't dye my eyelashes anymore so I use mascara, and I am always searching for something thicker and more effective, preferably a waterproof formula, such as Le Volume de Chanel. Make Up For Ever also has an amazing Aqua Eyes pencil that I can use if I want to add a bit of liner on my lower lid.

♥ I finish with eyebrow mascara from M·A·C. I love what Terry de Gunzburg, founder of the By Terry makeup line, had to say about it: "Redesign your eyebrows with a brow mascara and you'll get another look: Ava Gardner style. It automatically gives you the attitude that comes with it."

♥ For me, foundation is not the best product to use, but if I am in the mood, the brands that suit my skin best are Shiseido, which needs to be applied with a sponge, or Armani Fluid Sheer No. 11, which gives a wonderful glow.

♥ I am a fan and faithful devotee of Bobbi Brown Illuminating Bronzing Powder, and I play with it depending on the day and what I'm going to be wearing. On top I add a powder blush on my cheekbones from Bobbi Brown as well. Sometimes, instead of a bronzing powder, I use Dior Capture Totale Dreamskin Perfect Skin Cushion followed by a Chubby Stick from Clinique for my cheeks or a liquid blush from Armani called Fluid Sheer.

♥ The colors I choose for my lipstick are never too vibrant. I use Chanel, Dior, or By Terry lipsticks and apply them very lightly; because I already put on strong eye makeup, I keep my lips more subtle. A famous makeup artist once told me that one should never accentuate two areas of the face, and I choose to accentuate the eyes.

MY GRANDMOTHER'S MAKEUP ROUTINE

Maturité

My grandmother is well known for her lovely red lipsticks; she'll never leave the table after a meal without first retouching her lips! Now, as she is happy to point out, her makeup routine is much simpler than it used to be and is ideal for all women *d'un certain âge*.

RÉGINE: As you grow older, the skin has a tendency to become dull and the spots are more visible, so it is important to smooth the complexion. You may use various shades of concealers, but make sure your skin is well moisturized before starting. Light beige works for de-pigmentation and dark rings under the eyes as long as they are not too dark. For blue circles, use an orange-yellow shade. A green shade eliminates redness. The different shades of beige help to get rid of the tired look, and the light purple shade works on brown spots.

After the concealers, I apply my foundation. I always choose one with a very light texture, such as those from Shiseido, to avoid adding weight to my thinning skin. I use a product adapted to my needs and apply the foundation with a sponge or a brush for a delicate application that will not alter the first step of concealing I have just done.

Next, I add a little blush to add some luminosity to my face. I usually avoid darker shades of blush now, but in the summer months I still love to add a bit of Bobbi Brown bronzer.

For the eyes and eyebrows, I reshape my eyebrow line with a pencil to balance and enhance the look. I use a black mascara, although shades of brown are usually recommended, as they are less harsh. I must admit I am still very partial to mascara. I like to put it on lightly at the end of the lash line because it gives a youthful look, which seems to lift the gaze.

I finish off with a lip pencil of the exact same color as my lipstick for contour. I apply it by touches to fix the lipstick; it helps define my lips and keeps the color from feathering. I adopted lighter and brighter shades, as darker ones made me look older. The lipstick itself isn't too greasy, because when you grow older you get a few fine wrinkles around the mouth, so you need to be careful that lipstick doesn't crease.

Nowadays, makeup is a lot more natural. In my time, we were obviously "made up" and powdered. Compact blush and bronzer, for example, did not exist when I started modeling, and they give you a much lighter appearance than powder. As I've gotten older, I'm glad that the textures give me the same coverage without being quite so heavy. I've learned that as you get older, your skin doesn't absorb makeup as well—it has a tendency to remain on the surface rather than be absorbed by the skin. After menopause, when your skin becomes drier and loses elasticity, you need to adapt your makeup routine to minimize the signs of aging and still get that lovely radiance of youth.

Another thing that didn't exist back then was the ease with which you can find expert advice now, because when I started modeling in 1947, we didn't have makeup artists or hairdressers; we did it all ourselves. I often shared a dressing room with Irving Penn's wife, Lisa Fonssagrives, but she was a bit older, so we didn't have quite the same look. There were no cover girls until the film *Cover Girl* with Rita Hayworth was released in 1944. It was Americans who started that. It did not exist in France. In France, we had models *en cabines*—the house models for the couturiers who showed the new season's dresses to the clients—who posed for photographers.

In the 1950s, liquid eyeliner did not exist, so we had to use a thick pencil instead. The result was not as nice and meticulous as what you can do with the eyeliner we have today. Yves Saint Laurent mascara, which I love, did not exist then, so we all used Rimmel, which was extraordinary. But the mascara back then didn't come in a tube—it was a pressed cake, and you had to use saliva to make it liquid enough to apply with a brush. This gave you a *formidable* result.

We used loads of powder back then, too, especially from T. LeClerc and Caron. They were very reputable brands. First, I would use a clarifying toner from Elizabeth Arden or Orlane in the morning. Once it dried, I would apply a light liquid cream as a moisturizer. I then applied loose powder in order not to shine; in those days, one absolutely couldn't have shiny skin. One had to be matte. We never used brushes with our powder; instead, we had these enormous, wonderfully soft powder puffs made from swan down. We would carefully apply the powder to our faces and our necks; it was *the* must-have makeup item of the 1940s and 1950s!

I also learned from the Carita sisters that if you want your makeup to last for a long time, you should not put heavy or oil-based creams on your face. A light cream is best; today we would use a serum. Otherwise, as the hours pass in the evening, the excess moisture will remain on the surface of your face and you will not have the dewy look you're after.

"Bourjois: Not Only French, but Parisian!"

That was the claim in a Bourjois advertisement in *The New York World* in 1922—how true it was then, and still is!

I have vivid memories of the wonderful day when I bought my first Bourjois blushes—I was only a teenager, and my friends and I were obsessed by the adorable little round jars they came in. They reminded us of *macarons*! Prices were affordable, and the neighborhood store that sold them had this huge display with all their products. It was so colorful and attractive.

Years later, I read *Bourjois Paris—Beauty with a French Accent Since 1863* by Valérie Vangreveninge and Elisabeth de Feydeau, a book which describes the origins of the brand. "The first Bourjois beauty kit was aptly named the 'Ladies' Friend.' It slid easily into evening bags to be proudly shown off in public. Even then, the Bourjois extra touch was undeniable: the compact's lid contained a mirror! And thus began the great journey of clever Bourjois products . . ."

THE BEST WAY TO LEARN WHAT MAKEUP SUITS YOU IS TO TAKE A LESSON

LORRAINE: Years ago, a friend quite bluntly told me that I wasn't doing my eye makeup correctly. "Your eyeliner is not properly applied and could look better," she declared, much to my embarrassment. "Ask a pro for advice. You'll look so much better!"

I suppose she could have been a little less direct, but she actually did me a huge favor, because I decided I was long overdue to take a few makeup classes. Even though my mother was an expert at doing her own face, I had different ideas about what I wanted on mine, and I honestly had never had anyone sit down and teach me.

So I went to see Christine at Carita Montaigne, who I had known since I was eighteen years old when she did the makeup of my Parisian debutante party hosted by my parents at Le Moulin de la Galette. At the time, she was just starting her career. First, she asked me what kind of looks I preferred, and then she did one side, talking me through each step, and then supervised as I did the other side. I was amazed at my instant transformation. Instead of very basic eyeliner, I learned to redesign the line of a black eyeliner or a black eye crayon, and, most of all, to apply the eye shadow in the crease going outward in a taupe color, which I did not know how to do before. It instantly opens up and widens the look. It is more of an evening look, but of course it depends on the intensity of the eye shadow that I learned to play with depending on the time of the day. Even better, my new makeup routine was so quick and infallible, as Christine says, "Doing your makeup is like cooking from a new recipe. If you only do it once, you will never learn. The more you do it, the better you get until it becomes completely natural."

All the makeup artists I interviewed for this book agree that if your makeup teacher is good, a makeup lesson can be incredibly beneficial. It's also cost-efficient in the long run, as you won't be making impulse buys and wasting your money on products that you know won't suit you.

The best way to find the right makeup artist is to ask around or to go to the beauty counters at a department store. Many of them have trained makeup artists on staff, and the lesson is almost always free (although you might want to buy a product as a thank-you). Look for staff who have done their makeup in a way you like. It might take some experimentation to find the perfect artist, but that's half the fun.

As my mother says, "Following the advice of a good makeup artist is priceless, and you will be given a gold mine of tips that you can take back home. Experts will know how to use and blend colors for your specific skin tone—this is an art and not something that most of us are good at. So they can really help you."

A Few Words About Eyebrows

As my mother is fond of saying, you should never take tweezers to the start of your eyebrow line, since it is the true definition of your brows and it gives you character.

It is tempting, of course, to get a little overzealous and tweeze or wax a bit too much at times. If you removed too much of your eyebrows, let them grow for three months to get them fully back to your normal, natural shape. Use tweezers with a diagonal angle to follow the eyebrow line and give it a direction.

If your eyebrows are sparse, use an eyebrow pencil to color them discreetly. Otherwise, go for mascara for eyebrows, which offers good results, even if it is temporary.

The Ideal Eyebrow Grooming Kit
- Clear mascara (Glossier)
- Eyebrow mascara in a shade that matches your coloring (By Terry)
- Laura Mercier Sketch & Intensify Pomade and Powder Brow Duo in Brunette
- Kevyn Aucoin and Sisley Paris Phyto-Sourcils Design pencils
- A good pair of tweezers (Vitry)
- A brush specially made for eyebrows (M·A·C, Bobbi Brown)

THE MAKEUP TOOLS YOU'LL ALWAYS NEED

Before you think about putting your makeup on, it helps to have the right tools. They make an enormous difference in your application—which you will have learned from a makeup artist. They are inexpensive and last for a long time.

Basically, all you need are sponges and brushes of various sizes (small for eye shadow, eyeliner if you use it, and lips; larger for foundation and blush) and tweezers. The tweezers I prefer are by Vitry, a French company that's been making them since 1795.

Just as with colors, play around with different brushes and

brands—you'll know which one is right for you when it feels good and is easy to manipulate when you're holding it.

One of the best makeup tips I have ever gotten is from makeup artist Muriel Baurens: "It's worth going to art shops for your brushes, as they come in all sizes and prices. Because the second you wash a cheap brush with soap and water, the bristles fall out."

Makeup artist and Creative Director for Guerlain Olivier Échaudemaison shares the sentiment: "Older formulations of foundation were quite heavy, so makeup artists started using sponges. I personally prefer brushes for spreading foundation—for me, the skin becomes a canvas.

"When you are applying blush or bronzing powder, the bigger the brush, the better to diffuse the powder. It is better to have to add layers rather than just applying one thick coat, because then you run into the problem of streaking."

I personally like to use both sponges and brushes. The sponges that work best for my foundation and any tinted creams are by Clé de Peau and Shiseido. For brushes, I love Bobbi Brown and Antonym.

Makeup Brushes and Sponges Need Regular Cleaning

Wash brushes often in warm, soapy water, or swirl them around in warm water with a bit of gentle shampoo in it. Rinse well. Do not dry them upright, as this lets the water drip down into the handles and can warp them over time. Squeeze out as much water as possible, move the bristles back into place, flattened, and air-dry.

For sponges, makeup artist Christine from Carita says, "First soak your sponge in a soapy solution to loosen and break up

Régine Debrise. This photo was Irving Penn's first French *Vogue* cover.
Photograph by Irving Penn © Conde Nast. Vogue October 1950.

Régine Debrise in Balenciaga. *Photograph by Irving Penn © Conde Nast. Vogue September 1950.*

Régine Debrise in Dior. *Photograph by Irving Penn © Conde Nast. Vogue*
September 1950.

Lorraine Bolloré by Jean-Daniel Lorieux.

French actress Isabelle Adjani by Guy Bourdin for French *Vogue*.
© *The Guy Bourdin Estate, 2017.*

Photograph of Jacques Courtin-Clarins with Lorraine Bolloré at a press event in Paris.

Photograph of Estée Lauder with Lorraine Bolloré at an event in New York.

Le Prix Jasmin by
Daniel Jouanneau.
© *Daniel Jouanneau.*

Lorraine Bolloré at the
Dior Poison perfume
launch "Bal Poison."

Clémence von Mueffling by Pamela Berkovic.

makeup, then spot-clean and rinse thoroughly. Lay them flat and let them air-dry."

All Your Beauty Needs Can Be Found at Le Bon Marché, the Parisian Temple of Beauty and Fashion

The very first *grand magasin* (department store) in the world opened its doors in 1852. Located between the chic 6th and 7th arrondissements, Le Bon Marché has become the symbol of the Rive Gauche and its *art de vivre*.

Any occasion to be back in Paris is always good. And it was no exception when I had the chance to pay a visit to Le Bon Marché and have the pleasure of meeting Marie-Françoise Stouls, the talented head of the beauty department. This woman knows beauty. She first began working at Le Bon Marché in 1979 and took charge of its beauty department in 1992, and she has had to rethink their strategy in the challenging context of today's competition. For this, she turned to New York for advice since the department stores there were way ahead at the time in terms of positioning and marketing the many beauty lines they offered to consumers. One of her initiatives was to be the first to bring Bobbi Brown to France while still representing the classic cosmetics brands.

According to Marie-Françoise, the biggest revolution in makeup in the last few years has been not only the choice of colors but also in the modernity of textures (lighter and more fluid while providing full covering power) and more natural products, not to mention the array of tools such as brushes, pencils, and sponges.

"Before you choose the best makeup for yourself, it is most important to always have a good makeup removal routine," she told me. (I think you know this by now!) "Even though a touch of blush can always improve your complexion, what you really want is beautiful skin thanks to your regular cleansing routine."

Although it is located in Paris, Le Bon Marché (and now its website, 24 Sèvres) has become an international symbol of Parisian style and elegance.

Makeup Is Not Forever!
A few words of wisdom from Elisabeth Bouhadana about your makeup's use-by date:

There are different categories of products; some you use directly on the skin, like lipstick. So there is a direct contact between the product and the lips, and there is a rather positive bacterial ground in place there. However, because there is no water in lipstick, there's less chance for bacteria to grow. And even if there is some bacteria on the lipstick, this should be okay and the lipstick can last a very long time. If, however, it smells off, or rancid, toss it immediately.

With foundation, it's not the product itself but the applicator, the sponge, or the brush you use. At each application, some dead cells, sebum, and residues are going to end up on the applicator, so you need to clean or use a new one after each use because it's a breeding ground for bacteria.

For eyeliners, it doesn't really matter because they are calibrated in such a way that if you use them daily, within a month and a half, the product will be entirely used.

You should *never* use testers in stores. You have no idea whose fingers have touched them already! (Fortunately, stores like Sephora now have Q-tips, tissues, and cleansers at their makeup counters for more hygienic testing.)

In general, you should always wash your hands before you apply cosmetics, and you should clean your face thoroughly in the evening even if you don't use makeup.

Some people who live in warm climates store their creams in the fridge, but if you have air-conditioning, it doesn't really matter. What matters is the variation of temperature. Keep all your skincare products away from heat and light.

The Best Tips from Two of France's Top Makeup Artists

Olivier Échaudemaison, Creative Director for Makeup at Guerlain, began his career as a hairstylist with Alexandre de Paris, the "hairstylist to the stars" in the 1960s, where he used to watch Twiggy and the other cover girls of the era do their own makeup. He would soon become their favorite makeup artist, and he was hired to work on photo shoots for some of the world's most prestigious magazines and top photographers, such as Richard Avedon, Helmut Newton, Guy Bourdin, Norman Parkinson, and David Bailey. He's worked with some of the most beautiful women in the world: Grace Kelly, Audrey Hepburn, Sophia Loren, Ava Gardner, Jacqueline Kennedy, and Romy Schneider. The most beautiful face he's ever seen? The incomparable Elizabeth Taylor.

What made me a makeup celebrity in the 1970s was that Norman Parkinson, who was one of the best-known photographers for the

British royal family, asked me to accompany him on an anonymous photo shoot—because I am French—to Buckingham Palace for the first official photo of Princess Anne, the daughter of the Queen of England, who was twenty-one at the time. After that, I went on to do her engagement photos, from the engagement to her wedding, from the marriage to her children. I was very discreet about it, as the royals didn't want the press to know that Princess Anne was using a French makeup artist. Quiet word still got out, which gave me fantastic publicity in the aristocratic circles of Europe, and suddenly all the princesses were asking me to do their makeup. I also worked quite a lot with Jacqueline Kennedy as her hairdresser and her makeup artist, because back then there were very few professional makeup artists outside of Hollywood.

The French and European way is that they don't wear very much. A bit of this and a bit of that. Whereas Asians, for example, specifically Japanese women, like their makeup to be seen. With American women, it's one or the other. Either the look is completely natural, with little to no makeup, or the other side of the spectrum: completely done up. There's no real in-between.

The French don't like looking like they are wearing makeup. They do everything possible so that their skin looks flawless, and they care for their skin well, so their makeup is imperceptible. However, the French do like to show a certain sensuality. So red lips—but not aggressively so. Nails are often colored, especially the toes. So there is a bit of color, but on the eyelids, not really. Taupe, beige, gray, etc., but no green or turquoise or bright colors. Your eyelids are not rainbows. Eyebrows? Yes. No fake eyelashes. Eyebrow tinting? Yes. And mascara. French women, Parisian women, won't go out without mascara and lipstick. There is a form of sophistication from lipstick. It took a while for people to understand that it is an accessory according to the season, the time of day, and so on. It's like matching a bag to your shoes. But as a general rule, French women try to make their makeup look as real as possible. They don't want to look alike or like anyone else they know. There isn't so much of a cult culture where French women want to look like celebrities.

How Makeup Has Evolved

One of the advantages these days is the texture of the makeup. Before, texture was difficult. Today, we can have almost invisible texture, especially with foundation, which still delivers results. The most important thing is good skin. The first thing to work toward, no matter what age and generation, is to have nice skin. Luminous skin. The skin reflects who you are, what you eat, all that you do. And I have many clients who like to make believe that they don't smoke! There is no mystery to it—I can see very well when a woman with no makeup is a smoker or nonsmoker.

Olivier Échaudemaison's Golden Rules

- ♥ The best way to prime your skin for makeup is to drink lots of water to eliminate toxins throughout the day.
- ♥ When applying makeup, you need to have a light hand! You don't need four layers of mascara. Same with foundation.
- ♥ In your twenties and thirties, you can do it all. No makeup, exaggerated makeup, whatever you like. But I believe that when you reach *un certain âge* you should avoid using too much.
- ♥ At forty, French women basically know what suits them, and will maybe use a little bit less makeup. They all want to look younger, because these days, they *can* look younger than they are without doing Botox.
- ♥ At sixty, French women don't go out without makeup. Because luminosity has diminished at this age, the skin does not have its previous elasticity. But one must do this with a light hand

to keep one's finesse. So light colors, no black. Use navy blue or brown, which makes for a lighter look. A twenty-year-old woman looking at a fashion show can wear the Martianlike makeup she sees. At that age, you can try everything. But an older woman can't.

♥ For all ages, lipstick will always work. I don't see one Hollywood star or celebrity who goes out without lipstick. There is something magical about it—it's the number-one product to bring on a desert island.

♥ If you are going out at night, especially right after work, put powder on your T-zone. That is important because that area should never shine; it should always be matte. If you want your makeup to stay on and look great from seven p.m. to two a.m., a heavy day cream should be avoided, especially if you are drinking champagne! Pay attention to the texture of creams—it's always about the texture! If you have a creamy cream, you must apply powder after. Too much powder, however, can look streaky, so use a light powder.

♥ Also, at night, avoid colors that are too aggressive on eyelids as well. In the daytime, turquoise, white, or dark blue work. But at night it is hard. A very bright lipstick might be too much to go to the neighborhood bistro for dinner. But if you have red toenail polish, why not add a little transparent color between lipstick and gloss, something like a colored lip balm. That looks really nice, because lip color makes your eyes shine. And your smile, of course, makes everything shine.

♥ Remember that light changes throughout the day: sunlight, artificial light, etc. Makeup worn during the day won't look the same at night. You need to not just evolve with the time and day but think of the season, too. Makeup has that advantage: frivolity. It is not necessary, but it is *indispensable.*

Christine from Carita Montaigne, Makeup Artist Since 1969

Christine began her career as a makeup artist at Carita Montaigne when she was nineteen, and she is still going strong! She's spent her entire lifetime making French women look their beautiful best. Here are her best tips:

Some women love a sophisticated look; others like a more natural look. In this generation, women tend to like what looks like subtle makeup. But all these celebrities and Instagram stars in fact wear loads of makeup, which isn't possible to do on a daily basis. That is the contradiction. They say they want a natural look and when they show photos of the desired look, it's always a heavy makeup. Contouring, for instance, is an effort. It's great for photos, but not for everyday life. Smoky eyes also take a long time. And the effort to keep it looking that way is important to note as well! It's easily smudgeable.

My favorite tools are good brushes, and I use the ones from Make Up For Ever because there is a lot of choice.

To keep your makeup on as long as possible, avoid greasy or heavy creams. I love serums. They're perfect for a flawless look under your foundation. And then put a powder on—with a sponge! Because applying powder with a brush does not matte the skin at all. Also, long-stay foundation can leave traces by the end of the day, so I prefer normal foundation. Apply powder after. For eye makeup, powder eye shadow and a kohl eyeliner will last the longest. Try to avoid waterproof mascara, as it is difficult to remove, and over time the excessive rubbing you need to do will weaken your lashes. And fake eyelashes, because they can leave your real lashes very weak. If you tint your eyelashes, however, they will look good for a long time.

To transition from day to night, take a cotton pad—with *no* cleanser on it. Blot your lips to remove any excess color, and then swipe gently over your eyelids to do the same. This leaves a bit of color, which acts as a primer. Add to it. It holds longer. If you start from zero, it doesn't hold as long. I never take off my makeup then reapply it if I am going out after. However, I obviously take it off before going to bed!

It is so important to do your eyebrows, and we forget that. They frame your face. Basically, work on everything that opens up your eyes.

I like putting a lighter foundation under my eyes, instead of the usual under-eye concealer, because that can be too thick.

If you aren't happy with the texture of your skin, avoid powder. Blend your foundation with your fingers. I usually blend different foundation colors so they become a perfect match.

When you regularly wear makeup, you get used to its feel and are naturally more careful about it. A woman who only wears makeup once in a while is less used to feeling it on her skin, so she is more likely to touch her face and then wonder why there are smudges!

Removing Hair from Your Face

Unwanted hair, especially on the face, is one of those embarrassing problems that is difficult to discuss. French women tend to go for waxing at their local *institut de beauté*, where hair removal becomes as commonplace as a facial.

As women grow older and go into perimenopause and then menopause, they can start having unusual facial hair growth. Endocrinologist Catherine Brémont-Weill explains why:

With menopause, the female hormones (estrogen and progesterone) decline, and the male hormones, or androgens, that all women have in much smaller amounts, become stronger. The sensitivity to androgens on some areas of the face can lead to facial hair growth on or around the chin or the lips. This problem can be addressed with the use of hormone replacement therapy, after making sure there are no medical contraindications to it.

Other methods of cosmetic dermatology can work according to the nature and color of the hair, such as lasers or electrolysis. You may talk to your doctor to see if the prescription cream Vaniqa is right for you. This is a cream that slows hair growth, but it only works as long as you keep using it.

Other options include gentle waxing or threading. Avoid bleaching, as that is very harsh on tender skin. Colette Pingault, founder of the Adrienne Institut de Beauté, suggests that you use Cicalfate by Avène after waxing to help soothe your skin.

There are two permanent solutions for hair removal: electrolysis, which uses a fine needle that sends an electric current to the hair follicle, destroying it; or lasers. Electrolysis is still the only permanent way to remove hair from your face, but it is time-consuming and painful. Lasers are effective only on dark hair, and they work best on lighter skin tones. If you decide to go for laser hair removal, make sure to have a consultation with a board-certified dermatologist or plastic surgeon first. Lasers can be very dangerous when used by those with little training, and they can leave permanent marks on skin.

Part Three

Le Corps

Chapter 7

Three Generations of Expert Advice on Body Care

There are no unattractive bodies; there are only bodies that have yet to be shaped.

—BÉATRICE ARAPOGLOU

*T*his was something I heard many years ago from Béatrice Arapoglou, my ballet and posture teacher—who is featured later on page 206 in Chapter 9—and I never forgot it. What I love so much about it is the positivity it carries, because it means that we can all improve what we were born with. Not only our posture with the appropriate work but our skin as well—as long as we use the right techniques and products.

Not so long ago, I went to a wedding and saw a friend there, wearing a beautiful dress with a totally open back. The honeytoned smoothness of her bare back was flawless, her posture impeccable, and I went home that night, inspired and determined to take even better care of my skin. She was an inspiration—as well as proof that body maintenance isn't just about improving your skincare routine before a vacation or a special event.

There are certain parts of the body that French women pay particular attention to: the décolleté, upper arms, hands and nails, and upper thighs (particularly due to cellulite), the veins on the legs, and the feet. Let's take a look at each of these in detail.

YOUR DÉCOLLETÉ

The décolleté is the area under your neck and between your breasts. Though often overlooked, in reality, it needs extra daily care and attention. That's because the skin of your décolleté is thinner and has fewer oil glands than the skin on other areas of your body, so it's more likely to become dry due to a lack of natural hydration—which means wrinkles can easily form. In addition, we often forget to put sunscreen on this area, and if we wear shirts with V-necks or that have a few buttons undone, well, skin damage can occur. Unfortunately, there are no effective treatments to address a dry, damaged, and wrinkled décolleté, so it's much better to be prepared and take the proper precautions.

Jeunesse

Your skin should still be smooth and supple, but this is the time when you need to get into the habit of always wearing a high-SPF sunscreen on any exposed skin. Let it soak in before you get dressed so it doesn't rub off on your clothes.

Plénitude and *Maturité*

♥ Hopefully your skin will not show too many signs of damage, and your sunscreen habit is as ingrained as brushing your teeth!

♥ The harsh minerals in tap water dry and irritate your skin, so avoid taking showers in very hot water. Be mindful to blot your skin, rather than to rub when towel drying, to prevent damaging capillaries.

♥ Be sure to moisturize your décolleté after spending time in the sun and immediately following a shower or bath. Any rich cream or oil is suitable.

♥ In the evening, my number-one rule for my décolleté is to include it in my cleansing routine. So when I use a toner on a soft cotton pad for my face, I also swipe it across that area.

♥ Sometimes I feel I have applied too much moisturizer to my face, so with a flat hand I gently "stretch" the product on my décolleté. Otherwise, I use my body lotion and apply it, always with the whole palm of my hand, bringing the product from the center to my upper right shoulder and then back to the center and then to my upper left shoulder.

Our Favorite Body Creams and Oils

Jeunesse: Malin+Goetz Vitamin B5 Body Moisturizer; The Body Shop Coconut Oil Body Butter; Soapwalla Citrus and Almond Body Oil.

Plénitude: Avène Body Oil, Bioderma, Leonor Greyl oil, Caudalie Vine Body Butter.

Maturité: Environ Enhanced A, C & E Oil; La Roche-
Posay Lipikar.

TAKING CARE OF YOUR UPPER ARMS

Lax skin on the underside of your upper arms is something French women dread. For many women, this area of the body is as sensitive as the décolleté in terms of their care routine.

Often called bat-wings or bingo-wings, this area not only needs a lot of moisturizing—as the skin there has a lower level of oil glands to keep it hydrated—but is hard to tone unless you do regular arm exercises that strengthen the triceps as well as the other muscles. Be sure to moisturize your arms with a rich cream or oil after every shower, bath, or day at the beach.

LORRAINE: How can we remedy this? I have seen many women lately who prepared for this problem by working out their upper arms, and I realized you are never too old to start doing a sequence of exercises to firm them; I've seen great results with dance classes and gym routines.

According to Christophe Marchesseau, a licensed masseur-physiotherapist, and the founder of the Physio-Spa concept, the best sports to tone the upper arm are swimming, walking with poles, and biking. My advice is to hire a professional trainer for a lesson with small hand weights that you can easily use by yourself every day at home. Exercises for this area need to be done with precision or you won't achieve the desired results, so getting expert training will allow you to do them properly and see real results.

PERFECT UP TO YOUR FINGERTIPS

With all the treatments available to remove wrinkles and other signs of aging from our faces, women often forget about their hands. Without good care, however, hands are unwittingly a dead giveaway of your true age.

In past centuries, such as during the Renaissance, a woman's hands were considered a distinctive sign of beauty—aside from the face, hands were the only part of a woman that was visible while wearing formal court attire. (The French beauty treatises of the time would say, "When the gloves are off, the hands must express the sensibility and refinement of a woman.")

Since we rarely wear gloves now, except when it's cold outside, we need to take extra care and not neglect our hands. I have to admit that this is one area I need to constantly remind myself about—especially to keep my hands well hydrated. This means stashing hand cream near my computer at work, in my handbag, and on my nightstand at home so I can apply it regularly.

You also don't want to have lovely, hydrated skin whose appearance is ruined by raggedy nails, of course. Regular manicures not only maintain nail shape but nail health. As my grandmother would say, "If you find a talented manicurist where you live, keep her!"

RÉGINE: At French *Vogue* during the haute couture shows, we used to host beauty editors from American *Vogue* who were also covering the collections in Paris. In the early 1950s, American beauty editors were incredibly sophisticated. My French colleagues and I would be particularly amazed at how beautifully dressed they were, with perfectly manicured, red lacquered nails. Even during those long, hard working days in Paris, running around the city to see the collections, it always impressed us so much how their nails remained impeccable throughout!

Here are some wonderful tips from two great experts so you can maintain youthful hands and gorgeous nails.

Manicurist Béatrice Rochelle on Taking Care of Your Hands and Nails

Béatrice Rochelle has been taking care of hands and nails of chic Parisians, both men and women, for nearly thirty years. She is one of the most famous manicurists in town, and she counts Catherine Deneuve as one of her longest and most faithful clients. Her youngest client is six, and her oldest is 104! When they arrive for their appointments, they know that they will be there for over an hour. *"Real* hand care takes time," Béatrice likes to tell them. "The nail should be returned to its original form, and this is not a speedy process!"

General Care for Your Hands

When washing your hands, use a gentle soap with a neutral pH, which cleans without stripping the skin, and dry your hands and nails well. If you get sick, try to avoid hand-sanitizing gels with high alcohol content, as they tend to dry up the skin. Instead, use a hydrating soap bar or gentle liquid cleanser.

As your hands age, the skin, which is already thin, becomes finer and wrinkles become more prominent. Start hydrating regularly. And relentlessly! I don't have any particular preference—just a rich cream that is super-hydrating. If you have nail problems, use a cream for your hands and an oil for your nails, as it penetrates the nail better.

Almond, jasmine, and lavender oil are good for your skin and will improve nail growth, too.

For extra hydration, when you use your body cream, rub the excess into your hands for extra moisturizing. When you are on vacation or if you are out in the sun, squeeze the juice of half a lemon into a container with a few spoons of olive oil, and let the warmth of the sun heat it. Put your hands in it and leave them for as long as you want.

Your diet is very important, too. You want to be sure your vitamin and mineral levels are good, especially all the B vitamins, zinc, and iron. You might want to see if beer yeast or brewer's yeast (a product of the fermentation of the gluten found in barley that contains biotin) supplements are helpful.

Manicure Tips

Don't push the cuticles too far back, because that damages the nail bed, which can make nails fragile and brittle. Some people produce a lot of skin around the nails, and by cutting it the *right* way, it doesn't grow back as aggressively. Only let a professional do this to your cuticles!

Only wear nail polish six out of seven days. After having taken off your nail polish with a remover that does not contain acetone, you must let your nails breathe for a day.

When you take off your nail polish, make sure you press the cotton down onto the nail for a few seconds in order for the remover to seep into the polish. The thinner the cotton, the better it is.

All the chemical products, hardeners, and so on are really bad for your nails. The nail needs to be flexible, and if you harden it too much, it is paradoxically easier for it to break. If the nail is dry, you need to hydrate it rather than harden it with any chemicals that will aggravate the dryness even more.

I recommend that you only use naturally nontoxic polishes such as the ones from Kure Bazaar, which have a good choice of colors and last a long time. Catherine Deneuve is known for using them.

Special Tips for *Maturité*

For the height of sophistication, you can apply foundation on your hands to cover signs of aging such as dark spots. The best way to do this is to apply a hydrating cream to your hands and let it soak in, then add a bit of foundation with a makeup sponge on the back of your hand for a perfectly even skin tone.

If you are considering more advanced procedures to rejuvenate your hands, laser treatments can be used to smooth the skin and reduce pigmentation spots. To plump up hands, you can try injections of a filler like concentrated hyaluronic acid or your own fat (this is called a fat transfer). To reduce the appearance of veins, you would need to consult a phlebotomist and might need surgery.

Meilleur Ouvrier de France Aesthetician and Makeup Artist Sylvie Ferrari with More on How to Take Care of Your Hands and Nails

In France, we believe that workers in all industries are worthy of praise and distinction from their peers. This diploma and title belongs to the finest craftsperson in their profession, who must show expertise in contemporary as well as past techniques, and includes all fields of beauty treatments: face, body, nails, hands, feet, hair removal, and makeup. There is no proper translation for the title of *Meilleur Ouvrier de France*; suffice to say that it represents excellence in all of the above-mentioned fields. Sylvie is so popular that she even had a client coming for her weekly manicure accompanied by a little French poodle, who would march out proudly afterward wearing the same color nail polish as its owner!

Basic Manicure Tips

If you are going to have a manicure at a salon, the highest hygiene standards must be maintained for the instruments and the environment, she explains. Your manicurist should also be able to offer different treatments corresponding to your needs. She should provide advice; walk you through the steps of a particular treatment; the work should be quality-oriented; and she should be aware of the new techniques and be able to present them to you. Plus, of course, her hands should be impeccable.

You need to take care of your hands and nails as soon as you see cuticles appear. This usually starts when you are a teenager. But do you need to cut your cuticles? Yes . . . and no! If you get regular manicures, there is no need to cut your cuticles. If you often use oils for cuticles, the nail contour will be nourished and there will be no need to cut them, either. Cuticles should be cut only when the nail contour is dry and dehydrated.

There might be several reasons for nail dryness: if your hands are often in water; if you use a lot of detergents; if there is a lack of care; if there is constant exposure to the elements, such as cold and wind in winter. That is why it is so important to use hand cream and apply oil on the nail contour regularly.

At-Home Manicures

Make sure to file your nails; apply oil to the nail contour and into your cuticles; use a hand cream; and, if you feel like using nail polish, use a base coat, then the color, and then a top coat. You really do need to apply a base coat, as it protects the surface of the nail and does not need to be colored. The top coat protects the nail polish and makes it shine.

When you file your nails, avoid the back-and-forth motion. Use a soft nail file and work from the outside toward the center of the nail.

When you're choosing a color, it should be in harmony with your skin tone. Feel free to play around with different colors for a little bit of originality, but keep in mind your overall style and who may be seeing it. A perfect compromise if you like less-classic colors is to use them on your toes and choose a neutral color for your hands.

Nail polish removers must be gentle and without acetone. To recognize a good nail polish remover, test it by applying it. If your nail becomes white after application, it is not a good sign. It shows that the product is too strong.

To use nail polish remover properly, soak a cotton pad with nail-polish remover, place it on the nail and let the product work, then remove it horizontally—never from left to right or you will leave some polish on your skin.

Sylvie Ferrari's Manicure Kit

- ♥ A soft nail file
- ♥ Nail polish remover
- ♥ Cuticle oil
- ♥ Hand cream
- ♥ A serum or brightener to prevent dark spots (apply it regularly)
- ♥ Her favorite nail polish brands: OPI, Kure Bazaar, Essie, and Alessandro International

Jeunesse

Get a manicure on a regular basis and follow up by using a hydrating hand cream. When I go to get a manicure, I have learned to say no to two things if I do not know the manicurist. No to gel manicures that are extremely difficult to remove without a lot of chemicals, and no to the aggressive pushing back of the cuticles.

Plénitude

Get manicures with specific treatments, such as hyperpigmentation prevention by using serums, masks for hands, and/or a paraffin bath, depending on the state of your skin. Complete the treatments at home.

Maturité

Follow the routine for *plénitude*, and always make sure your hands are protected with a serum or sunscreen to prevent dark aging spots whenever you go out in the sun.

Our Favorite Nail Polishes

For All Ages:

We are faithful devotees of Kure Bazaar and have been using their polishes ever since Béatrice recommended them to us. My grandmother wears Rose Milk, my mother wears Macaron, and I wear Vinyle. Opt for more natural brands like Kure Bazaar or Sundays. They truly make an enormous difference in the health of your nails.

BUTTOCKS, THIGHS, AND DEALING WITH CELLULITE

If your legs and buttocks remain dimpled and uneven, no matter how much you exercise or how much you weigh, cellulite is the reason. Cellulite is normal body fat trapped in connective tissue with nowhere to go but to push outward. Either you are lucky and will never have it, or you are genetically unlucky and wonder what you can do to get rid of it.

Getting Rid of Cellulite

In Paris, those in the know go to see Martine de Richeville, who created her unique Remodelage massage technique after studying psychology, Chinese medicine, and Rudolf Steiner's Eurythmic massage. Her signature treatment is designed to rid the body of bulges and the mind of stress. She can attain long-lasting results using only the power of her hands, and she believes that, yes, there is a genetic component to cellulite, but that a mechanical and manual intervention like her method can definitely help.

These are her tips that will help you manage cellulite:

A teenage girl must take care of her body around the time of puberty. Food must be balanced and sugar intake monitored because the hormones are undergoing a huge shift, and it takes a lot of time for your body and metabolism to adjust.

If the cellulite is linked to a circulation or lymphatic problem and if it is located on the lower body, it is important to improve the venous return by wearing support stockings. Always consult a specialist who can define the level of support needed, because a wrong level of support can do more harm than good.

Every action that can improve the venous return will help: Elevate your legs at night, and use a cream on your legs morning and night (apply with circular motion from the ankle toward the knee). Using a horsehair glove is a good way to improve circulation.

Foods that are rich in vitamin E and antioxidants have a positive effect on circulation. Avocado, berries, bell peppers, and leeks have diuretic properties. Avoid salt and salty foods, eat high-fiber foods to keep your bowels moving, and drink a lot of water (at least one and half liters each day).

Cardio exercise is recommended, as long as it isn't too intense, such as sprinting or any sudden kind of movement that can shock your system. Practicing a sport regularly is the best way to maintain a good physical and mental balance.

If you persevere, you *can* transform your body thanks to this type of method, as long as you maintain a balanced diet and exercise regularly.

THE VEINS AND CIRCULATION IN YOUR LEGS

Did you know that, in the seventeenth and eighteenth centuries, trendy aristocrats insisted on having blue lines painted on their temples and elsewhere on their pampered bodies to show the world that they had "blue blood"? That might have been the height of chic back in the day, but not anymore. The French are a bit *obsessed* with varicose veins and dread the thought of them! This is a topic that is rarely discussed in the beauty world, and I've found that none of my friends and colleagues have much knowledge of this topic even though it is an extremely common condition, especially during pregnancy, and one that worsens with age.

These two Parisian specialists shared their expertise:

Dr. Jean-Pierre Titon, Paris-Based Phlebologist and Vein Expert, on Varicose Veins

Varicose Vein Basics
Varicose veins are parasite or fake veins. Think of them like a rose; for a rose plant to be healthy, you need to trim the tiny branches and

keep the stem clean. These parasites are called *gourmands* (greedy). You need to get rid of them, as they trap the venous blood (which is dark red in color). Unlike arterial blood (which is brighter red) that carries oxygen to your cells, venous blood is meant to carry away the waste products of cellular metabolism. If this venous blood is trapped, it causes trouble: heavy legs, swelling, eczema, and itching; it is going to impair the process of healing if you have a wound, and it's going to lead to many other problems. So it is useful to treat the varicose veins to avoid these conditions.

Genetics are also an important factor. In France, seventeen million adults have varicose veins: fourteen million women and three million men. In 70 percent of the cases, the cause is genetic. There are other factors like obesity, pregnancy, etc. If you do have varicose veins, it is important to have regular check-ups once or twice a year.

Sometimes your veins show, and you wonder if it's normal or not. It's easy to check: If your veins show on one side but not the other, you have varicose veins. Varicose veins are not symmetrical whereas veins tend to run in similar areas. Also, varicose veins are bumpy, form zigzags, can have a spider's web aspect, and are not in a straight line.

What to Do About Varicose Veins

As far as lifestyle is concerned, you need to avoid wearing tight clothing or doing anything that can have an impact on blood circulation. You need to move a lot, walk a lot, and drink a lot of water, especially in the summertime. Avoid excessive heat, such as hot baths/showers, saunas, and sunbathing. Try to get used to lukewarm water. Do not walk barefoot on the hot sand on the beach. It's like being cooked at low heat! Walk in the water; it's much better. Lastly, extreme heat is as bad as extreme cold.

Exercise is important. A good one to do is pretend-pedal a bike with your legs up in the air. Swimming, yoga, and walking are the best activities. Golf is better than tennis.

What you eat and drink is important, too, of course. Do not drink too much sparkling water because it can cause water retention. Drink champagne and wine moderately; white wine can trigger high blood pressure. Keep your weight at a normal level.

If you have varicose veins, it's best to avoid heavy-duty massage with a lot of pressing and rolling, as this can make things worse. Lymphatic drainage is relaxing, but if you have a serious condition, it is not going to help.

At night, try to elevate your legs four to six inches, using a pillow.

The most typical treatments are either injections, lasers, or surgery, and sometimes a combination of the three.

Caroline Meyrignac, of Orthopédie Meyrignac, on Compression Socks and Stockings

After speaking to Caroline, who is the fifth generation in her family to work in this business, I never, *ever* travel anywhere without wearing compression socks!

Compression Socks and Stockings Basics

Every individual is born with a different venous system, and our daily life has also a great influence on it. Due to their hormones and pregnancies, women have a tendency to develop venous insufficiency. In general, this starts with some pain during the day, the appearance of telangiectasias (tiny blood vessels that cause threadlike red lines or patterns on the skin), pain in the evening and during the night, and a feeling of restlessness (cramps, need to move the legs), and/or swelling at the end of the day at the ankle and foot level.

The purpose of medical compression is to apply pressure to

the legs to improve the venous and/or lymphatic return to avoid complications like stasis (when the blood stagnates at the bottom of the legs because of dilated veins). I recommend wearing support or compression socks or stockings as a preventive measure, especially if you know you will be spending prolonged periods in a standing position and/or intermittent walking, or if you will be sitting for long periods either at your desk or while traveling.

We often talk about support stockings, but I prefer *compression*, to be more precise. Compression applies a constant pressure at rest as well as at work. Medical compression is a mechanical process. The strongest pressure is at the ankle. It works as long as you wear the socks or stockings—whenever you take them off, the effect is gone!

The best way to take care of your compression socks and stockings is to wash them after each use in warm water, using a neutral soap or laundry soap. Rinse thoroughly. Remove excess water with a towel, and finish drying away from heat. You may machine wash as long as you use the delicate cycle, warm water, and a gentle spin cycle. Do not use softener, and do not use the dryer.

If you are wearing the compression garment all day long, it decreases in efficiency by 30 percent. Washing tightens the fabric, and the compression is back to its full potential. If you wear and wash the garments daily, they should last for three to four months.

You can use a lightweight moisturizing cream or lotion before you put on the compression socks or stockings. This won't change the effectiveness of the garment, but stockings tend to slide down if you have dry skin.

How to Use Compression Socks and Stockings

There is no specific age to start wearing support socks or stockings for plane travel. If you have a tendency to suffer from swollen legs and have trouble putting your shoes back on after a flight, then it's time for support! And of course, people who are constantly traveling by plane should wear support socks or stockings even if they don't show any symptoms. That's because the risk of thrombosis (phlebitis) increases with the length of the flight. I recommend wearing compression socks or stockings for at least one hour before travel time and keep them on for another hour after arrival. Walk around as much as you can once you arrive at your destination. If you go to bed soon after your arrival, you can take off the compression socks or stockings since you will be lying down. Still, the longer you keep the compression socks or stockings on after travel by plane, the better. It is important to remember that phlebitis symptoms do not always appear right away; they can occur two hours after you've landed, and you remain at risk for up to eight weeks thereafter.

It is very important to try on the socks to make sure that they fit properly. I do not recommend the purchase of medical compression garments online—they're medical products and can only be effective if they fit you properly.

Movement is crucial! A sedentary life, especially sitting in front of the computer all day long, is a common sign of our times, but it is very bad for the legs as well as for the body in general. Phlebotomists recommend thirty minutes of walking per day. Try to take the stairs rather than the elevator, and find any opportunity to walk. Even if you don't have time to go to the gym, find ways to make a wellness routine an integral part of your day.

Take showers rather than hot baths. End your shower by spraying cooler water on your legs, especially your ankles and calves. It doesn't need to be freezing water—just cooler than what you just showered in.

Massage your legs in the evening with an aromatic essential oil that has draining properties, such as lemongrass, rosewood, geranium, or rosemary. (Never use aromatherapy oils at full strength;

dilute them in an inert base oil such as sweet almond or jojoba.) Start at the ankle level and move up along the side of your calves and thighs. You can also try a massage with a cooling-effect leg gel.

Avoid prolonged sun exposure. If you happen to be by the ocean, take walks on the beach and walk in the water up to the knee level. It is especially good for the muscles, and the water gives you a natural draining massage.

Keep Your Legs Soft and Smooth

My welcoming neighborhood salon saved so many of my weekends when I was a teenager. In France, women would rarely shave their legs or underarms, and lasers for hair removal had just been invented and the treatments were very expensive. So off to the salon we went for waxing. There is nothing worse than being invited to a party when you're seventeen and you have hair growing in all the wrong places!

After years now of living abroad, I was happy to have an excuse to be back in Paris and reunite with Colette Pingault, the founder of the Adrienne Institut de Beauté, where I used to go as often as I could. Colette and her sister owned this beauty salon for thirty years in the Madeleine area of Paris. Nestled in a courtyard, they were devoted pretty much exclusively to waxing, the *mal-aimée* of aestheticians. Their expertise was based on hair-removal common sense: Wax with the grain in order to remove it swiftly without breaking the hair and leaving any stubble.

They would use a recyclable wax at a low temperature, keeping it supple and thick yet able to dilate the hair follicle. One journalist said something along the lines of: "If you have easily manageable hair, go to any salon; if you have difficult hair, go to Adrienne!"

What I learned from them is that if you're thinking about hair removal, don't be too aggressive with your skin. Try to wax more instead of shaving. Redness is hard to avoid after waxing on hyperreactive skin. Applying a cornstarch-based powder is recommended before all warm wax, as it avoids redness, and sweating is more controlled. Apply Cicalfate Restorative Skin Cream by Avène after waxing, and stay out of the sun before and after a wax.

TAKING CARE OF YOUR FEET

One beautiful Saturday morning in Paris, my grandmother asked me to meet her to celebrate my graduation from high school. I was thrilled, because I'd spent all spring studying day and night for the *baccalauréat* exam that all French students dread. When I arrived at the address she had given me on the rue de Bassano, I was surprised to see that it was the Revlon beauty salon—the most prestigious at the time. (Revlon is now a drugstore brand, but back then, it was definitely not over-the-counter in Paris!) I walked in to find my grandmother sitting in a bright and airy room with high ceilings, a sweet smile on her face. After I kissed her on the cheeks, she told me she was treating me to the most elegant and sophisticated *beauté des pieds*, as we call it in French. This is not just a "beautiful foot" pedicure—it was more of a medical treatment that uses special tools to clean, soften, and shape the nails so they would always grow out beautifully.

I felt so grown up, being pampered like that, and looking around the room at the impossibly chic ladies, who were chatting away with their regular aestheticians. My grandmother was one of their first clients in 1947, when their salon opened, and she continued to visit them once a month until it closed. She always says that the only reason her feet look so perfect today is thanks to the amazing professionalism of their aestheticians.

There are several different levels of treatments for feet. For any medical issues, you should first go to a podiatrist, who is a licensed physician with specialty training in caring for feet.

Next there is a medical-grade pedicure, and French women are very fond of them. During this kind of pedicure, calluses and cracks are diligently attacked by a highly trained professional, staving off problems that can arise from ill-fitting or uncomfortable shoes. They're a great option for nail care (especially ingrown nails, discoloration, ridges, infections, fungus) and skin of the feet (calluses, cracks in the heel area, corns, rough spots). They're usually done on dry skin.

Finally, there is the typical pedicure done in nail or beauty salons—like a manicure for your toes. It's usually done on moist skin and includes a peel or scrub.

Podiatrist Bastien Gonzalez on Treatments for the Feet

Bastien has become famous worldwide for his glamorous and unique approach to foot treatments. "Feet evolve throughout life," he explains. "If you could place four women from different generations of the same family next to each other, you would see how small deformations become larger ones over time. I would give the same advice: If you are under thirty-five, concentrate on prevention; if you are fifty and older, concentrate on treatment. That being said, age is not always a factor to consider. I have already had twenty-five-year-old supermodels as patients, who have very damaged feet as they've had to wear high heels every day at work, as well as women who are seniors yet still have feet like babies— thanks to their luck at having good genes and/or the way they've taken care of their feet over the years." This is his expert advice:

Once a month, use a scrub on your feet while showering.

As often as possible, massage your feet for a few minutes before going to bed to hydrate, stimulate the circulation, and help with the mobility of your joints. Do not forget to massage between the toes and the heel. Always use a foot cream, as the skin of your feet is much thicker than your face and needs special care.

Use an old electric toothbrush to clean the area on the side of the toenail, which will help remove any dry or dead skin and keep the area soft.

If you are not expert, then you should not cut your cuticles. But don't push the cuticles back too aggressively, either, as this leaves the door open for bacteria, and you risk infections.

After you push the cuticles backward, apply a daily cuticle oil, ointment, or cream to maintain hydration. Also avoid blades like peelers, as they can cut the skin due to their imprecise blades—they're different from the instruments used during medical-grade pedicures that use sterile surgical blades.

If you like nail polish on your toes, remove and change it every four or five days. Leaving it on longer isn't good for your nails.

A good habit is to use talcum powder in your shoes. It acts like invisible socks that reduce the friction in your shoes and keep your feet dry.

Gels, acrylics, and other nail products last between two weeks and two months depending on the quality of the product. These are made from harsh chemicals, and I do not recommend them. Although most people don't put fake acrylic nails on their toes, they shouldn't be used on your hands, either, as regular use causes the nail to become thinner and thinner as it's filed down, leading them to become softer and more prone to breakage.

Jeunesse

Be careful not to wear nail polish or gels, acrylics, and other chemical fake nails on a regular basis. Massage with a special foot cream regularly to be sure your feet get a good hydrating treatment. A squash ball can provide a good, simple, and efficient massage. Rolling the ball under the foot creates heat, which relaxes the intrinsic muscles of the foot.

Plénitude

Schedule a medical pedicure if you have corns, calluses, or cracks. Follow up with daily rubs with a rich hydrating cream. Slather it on and sleep with cotton socks, as this will allow the cream to penetrate without you slipping around or getting your sheets all creamy!

Maturité

Oftentimes, women want to have surgery for bunions or claw/hammer toes and the like. It is important to not have surgery unless the bunions are affecting how you walk or causing you pain. Surgery should be the last resort, as it is a painful procedure.

Giving Yourself a French-Style Pedicure at Home

Obviously, you can't do the kind of intense footwork a medical-grade pedicurist will do in a clinic or salon when you're at home—but unless you have specific foot-care needs that should be taken care of by a specialist, the simplest way to take care of your feet is to regularly do your own pedicures at home and use super-rich lotions and creams to keep your skin (and especially your heels) hydrated and smooth. Here's my technique for how to give yourself the best possible French pedicure:

♥ First, remove your old nail polish as recommended on page 139.

♥ During a warm shower or bath, scrub your feet well with a body scrub or one that is specifically made for feet. Massage them well with your hands, especially the areas that support most of your body weight, usually the areas that appear most damaged or that are sore, by doing a rotation movement. Don't be too vigorous! Then, dry your feet thoroughly, especially between your toes and your nails.

♥ Once the warm water has softened the skin on your feet, apply cuticle oil and massage it in for a minute. Then use a cuticle stick to gently push back the cuticles. This will make your toenails look neat and trim and will also help when you apply your nail polish. You can follow Bastien's suggestion to use an old electric toothbrush. Use it to brush the crease between the toenail and the skin.

♥ If your nails need to be cut, then wait until they are perfectly dry. I only use large nail clippers and avoid cutting nails into a round shape. They look best and grow best when they are square. It's best to make a few small cuts straight across, making sure you are not cutting them too short. This helps prevent ingrown toenails, which can hurt a lot!

♥ Filing is the same as for your fingernails. As per Sylvie's advice page 142, don't drag the file or emery board back and forth. Gently move the nail file in one direction across the top of your toenail until it's smooth and the appropriate length. You can also file/buff the top of the nail with a chamois nail buffer as recommended by Bastien to bring back the natural pinkish color to your toenails. He recommends applying a small amount of a buffing cream on the surface of each nail and rubbing vigorously with the nail buffer until no buffing paste is left.

♥ I finish by massaging the foot, toes, and especially the dry areas, such as my heels. If my feet are extra dry, I add a cream specifically made for feet directly onto the area in need of care. Massaging brings back their suppleness and relieves all the tensions accumulated during the day (especially if I wore high heels to a meeting or out to dinner!). I always start with the toes, then move to the arch of the foot, and finally, the heel. I finish up with a quick massage around my ankle, always keeping an upward movement.

My Pedicure Kit

♥ A scrub to remove dead skin
♥ A rich moisturizer for the feet, such as Aveda Foot Relief moisturizing creme, Neutrogena Foot Cream, or Révérence de Bastien Sensitive Feet Balm
♥ A large nail clipper
♥ A regular cuticle stick
♥ An old electric toothbrush
♥ A glass nail file with fine grains, such as Dr. Scholl's

or Révérence de Bastien; this is less stressful for your nails, as it won't file down the different layers

- ♥ A polishing/buffing kit: Deborah Lippmann buffer nail file or a chamois nail buffer and Révérence de Bastien's pearly buffing cream
- ♥ For nails and cuticles: Dior Crème Abricot Fortifying Cream For Nails, Elizabeth Arden Eight Hour Cream, Sally Hansen Cuticle Massage Cream, and Révérence de Bastien Unguent for Nails and Cuticles
- ♥ Talcum powder, to be used in the morning, after a shower, or before sports to help keep your feet dry
- ♥ Kure Bazaar or Sundays nail polish

What to Do When You Have Bunions

Orthopedic surgeon Dr. Serge Hautier has been famous for decades to those in the know in Paris. The number-one reason for a woman to visit an orthopedic surgeon for foot issues is due to bunions, which are a common deformity of the edge of the foot and near the big toe. They are often caused by genetic factors but can also be exacerbated by high heels (especially if you always wear them) as well as ill-fitting shoes. They often start with corns and calluses and can be incredibly disfiguring and painful. These are Dr. Hautier's recommendations:

To prevent corns and calluses and keep your feet healthy, I recommend sport shoes. They cannot be too tight, nor should they compress the foot.

The ideal height for heels is one and a half to a little over two inches in general, and up to three to four inches for special occasions.

Use foot cream regularly. You can easily find specific exfoliating creams to prevent calluses.

Surgery becomes necessary when the pain and deformity are severe. To limit the worsening of the condition and postpone surgery, comfortable shoes can be helpful in the short term, but the sooner you get surgery, the better. Bunions can't go away on their own.

After surgery, you should go to physical therapy sessions with cream-free massage. Avoid wearing tight shoes for three months.

You May Be Able to Avoid Bunion Surgery

Daniela Beccaria-Blamey is a SCENAR therapist and a registered member of the British Complementary Medicine Association and the Association of Energy Therapists. As she explains:

SCENAR (Self-Controlled Energo-Neuro Adaptive Regulator) is a biofeedback therapy that can reduce pain and inflammation and accelerate healing. It is used to treat a wide range of conditions that may affect different parts of the body and is particularly effective as a treatment for injuries as well as chronic inflammatory conditions, such as arthritis, bursitis—and bunions. A technician uses the SCENAR device to send electromagnetic signals via the skin that mimic nerve impulses; the device constantly measures the body's response and is able to adapt each signal accordingly. (This is what biofeedback does.) It's worth trying this technique, as it's pain-free and is suitable for all ages.

Part Four

Les Cheveux

Chapter 8

Beautiful Hair at Any Age

Hair has to have life and movement. It doesn't have to be perfect.

—DAVID MALLETT

When I first moved to New York, one of my best friends, who worked at Dior with me, took me out to a nightclub to celebrate. As we sat in a booth and watched the scene, the one thing that struck me more than anything else was how all the women in that club had the most amazing hair. It wasn't that they'd done it up or had used a lot of products—it was just different from French hair. So much thicker and shinier and full of volume. I thought about it all the way home, wondering what could account for such beautiful hair. Perhaps it was the water, because I had already learned that the water in New York City is "soft," and the water in Paris is "hard," meaning it has more minerals like calcium and magnesium in it. Water softness really does have an effect on your hair and skin, as they are less likely to lose natural oils in softer water.

But it had to be more than that, too. French women are often obsessed with hair care. They know, just as all women do, that hair is an incredibly important part of your identity. It's the first thing people see when you walk into a room. Stunning, shiny, healthy hair makes anyone happy; beautiful hair is like a necklace—you almost don't need makeup or any other pieces of jewelry or adornment when your hair looks great. A bad hair day—a phrase that doesn't exist in French, but should!—on the other hand, can instantly ruin your mood.

This is why French women often consult experts who can help diagnose and treat any issues, especially hair thinning and loss. While I admired that fullness of Americans' hair, I also recall that French women still manage to produce very attractive results. Let me explain.

RÉGINE: In the 1940s, movie stars influenced women into wearing their hair longer. L'Oréal was leading the pack for hair color and promised colorations with "natural" results. By the 1950s in France, many women were opting for shorter haircuts; it was becoming more *à la mode* to be functional and practical with hair as well as with clothing (which is why the Chanel suit was so popular). Salons started to become more and more comfortable, and French women flocked to them for perms and sets.

Yes, when I was younger, we always had to have groomed hair, particularly when we went out at night. Buns were fashionable, especially the "banana bun," named for its slightly oblong shape, which was timelessly elegant. This style is what made Alexandre so famous. Guillaume and Antoine were two other great hairdressers. Even though he was already in his eighties, Antoine, nicknamed Le Petit Prince, was in such high demand that he was able to open branches of his salon in America, especially after actresses like Audrey Hepburn, Sophia Loren, Ava Gardner, and Elizabeth Taylor were photographed in his salon.

It was always enjoyable going to a famous hairdresser—at Antoine's, I met Martine Carol, the French film actress, and Marlene Dietrich at Guillaume's. I still remember Marlene's hands; they were like porcelain, with nail polish the color of rose petals. Her nails were ravishing, and so was her hair!

LORRAINE: My generation in the 1970s and 1980s was the era when hairdressers went from being local stars to international trend-setters. Styles were changing at a rapid pace, and some of the French hairdressers were at the peak of their fame and success. Hollywood stars, French stars, and European socialites all wanted to have their hair done with the magical French touch. They'd go to see the Carita sisters, Rosy and Maria, and especially their nephew Christophe; Claude Maxime; Jacques Dessange; and of course Alexandre, nicknamed the king of hairdressers and the hairdressers of the kings!

In 1973, we were shooting a young, up-and-coming French actress named Isabelle Adjani for her first-ever beauty spread in French *Vogue*. At the time, she was only eighteen years old and starring in the play *Ondine* by Jean Giraudoux at the Comédie-Française, the prestigious Parisian theater. The photographer was the renowned Guy Bourdin, known for his sexually charged images—especially in advertisements—and his temper. The makeup was to be done by Heidi Morawetz. I had been told to book the hairdresser, Guillaume—but I had booked the wrong Guillaume. It was a disaster, and Guy was furious. It took me several hours to find the right Guillaume, who was actually Guillaume Bérard from Mod's Hair, who was a favorite with all the top fashion and beauty photographers. He was best known for a new sophistication with his hairstyles, which were less structured than the traditional French chignon. "We let the wind blow into our hair!" became one of my sayings, and I saw how hairstyles evolved from stiff and structured to what we call *coiffé-décoiffé*—hair that is done but does not look so done.

When Isabelle arrived, it was hard not to gasp, as she was so astonishingly beautiful, and still very young, in her late teens. Heidi knew that the best way to enhance Isabelle's looks was to actually do very little, as there was already so much intensity in her blue—almost purple—eyes, her very pale skin, and her masses of chestnut-brown hair. A touch of mascara, of blush, a purplish-red lipstick, and *voilà*! Guillaume then added some volume to her naturally curly hair, and the result was breathtaking. (The photo can be seen in the insert.)

A few years later, I had invited Isabelle, who was by then a movie star, to our home for lunch, and I told my older daughter, Raphaëlle, to be nice because there was a fairy arriving to eat with us. Isabelle was indeed a magical beauty who was totally enchanting even in her way of moving and talking. Raphaëlle really thought she was a fairy.

When I was sixteen years old, I wanted to straighten my hair because it was all the rage to have pin-straight hair, and there is no greater challenge than to keep a teenager from following a trend! My mother couldn't keep me from trying, but the heat and the processing did weaken my hair, and it left me with years of having to pay extra attention to treatments and conditioning. I often went to Carita's, as their essential oil and restructuring hair mask was particularly nourishing.

For a long time, I prepared my own shampoo: two egg yolks whipped up with a teaspoon of rum. For a final rinse, I used a liter of cold mineral water, with lemon juice or a few drops of Aceto da Toilette Violetta from Santa Maria Novella.

I also used castor oil for a while. I would cover my hair with it, put a shower cap on, and leave it on for an hour, which was not very practical or particularly lovely as far as smell is concerned! I then washed it out by shampooing my hair twice, as it is hard to remove. Remember that shampoos at that time were much harsher than many brands are today, and I don't know if the gentle, sulfate-free shampoo that I use today would be able to remove it easily.

Now, I sometimes apply coconut oil two hours prior to washing my hair, or even leave it on for an entire night and then wash it out in the morning. It leaves my hair very soft.

As for me, when I was younger, I was in awe of Brigitte Bardot's hair. She had pretty much started the craze for a new hairstyle named *saut du lit*. Her masses of naturally wavy and very thick blond hair always looked as if she'd just gotten up—or was giving you an invitation to go back to bed!—even if she'd been hard at work for hours. Nowadays, Bardot's au naturel style, with a simple layered cut and minimum time spent to get your hair just the way you want it, is the way to go.

For my generation and my friends, hairstyling has always been much more about getting a good cut than about experimenting with color or getting regular blow-outs. We started going to our neighborhood hair salon, just like we'd go to our neighborhood *pharmacie*, as there was usually at least one close by. I started with a simple haircut every few months to keep the tips of my hair healthy and to avoid split ends . . . until I was the unfortunate victim of the neighborhood hairdresser's newest hire, who was probably still in training and probably thought I was an ideal guinea pig to experiment on. In other words, he totally botched cutting my bangs. It was a complete disaster that my girlfriends still remember today.

After that very upsetting experience, I decided not to take any more risks. For example, I have always resisted changing the color

of my hair. I only very recently allowed the expert hands of Mar-
ris Ambrose, a talented colorist at Julien Farel's hair salon in
New York City, to color a few white hairs because I trust her.

Still, I didn't realize just how important the health of my own
hair could be until I started to have problems several years ago.
Usually, my hair is quite thick, and it suddenly changed texture.
It wasn't that I was losing my hair, but it became thin and never
looked totally clean. It was bizarre—it would look good for an
hour after I washed it, and then it would go totally limp and life-
less. I was so upset that I started using a headband that looks
like a braid made from your own hair, and it gave a false impression of volume. And then I counted the days until I would arrive
in Paris for a visit with my family, because I had made an appointment with a dermatologist specializing in hair, Dr. Barbara
Guedj. She told me I had a sort of psoriasis, which is sometimes
due to stress. I didn't think I was under stress at the time, but
sometimes you just don't know how life is going to have an effect on your body. She gave me some products to clean and heal
my scalp and some zinc to strengthen my hair. It only took a few
days for me to see improvement, and she helped me to feel so
much better about myself again.

So if you notice any changes in your hair, don't self-diagnose.
Get professional advice. You might be having a simple reaction
to a new shampoo, or a stress reaction like I had.

EXPERTS CHRISTOPHE ROBIN AND DAVID
MALLETT ON HAIR CARE

Christophe Robin and David Mallett have been two of the
most renowned hairdressers in France for decades and are syn-

onymous with great style, at times *au naturel* and always *à la mode*. Not surprisingly, these two wonderful men have many similar recommendations for your at-home hair-care routine:

♥ Don't wash your hair too often

Whether it's colored or not, washing your hair twice a week, no more, is what's best for most women. If you have to wash your hair on a daily basis because you are practicing a sport, or you do a lot of cooking, or you smoke cigarettes, or because of pollution where you live, try to use a cleansing cream or a sulfate-free shampoo, and remember to rinse thoroughly. "Do not shampoo twice; once is enough," Christophe says.

> **DAVID:** Overwashing is one of the things that causes all the problems with scalps, especially with hot water. It's better for the environment, it's better for your time, it's better for your scalp, it's better for your hair to wash it less. And it's better for your color.

♥ Rinse well

> **DAVID:** A big mistake that people make is that they don't rinse their products well enough, which can make hair flat, not shiny. You really have to rinse a product out of your hair, and *well*. Otherwise, no shine.

♥ Use mineral water

> **DAVID:** One of the most difficult things for hair is hard water. So if you wash it with soft water, mineral water, it's so much better at removing conditioner, and you'll see how beautiful and shiny your hair feels, and how good your scalp feels. It makes your hair look fantastic.

What's more, you can even do this at home if you have hard water where you live; it's not terribly expensive to use mineral water. Just do a final rinse of your hair with Evian and you'll have incredible shine.

♥ Make a do-it-yourself vinegar rinse

DAVID: My most favorite kitchen product is apple cider vinegar. I think it is one of the best products that you can use. It smells good. Get a one-liter bottle of Evian, put it in the fridge, get it completely chilled, add a small amount of vinegar, and rinse your hair with it at the end of your shower.

CHRISTOPHE: I like to use the fabulous Aceto da Toilette Violetta from Santa Maria Novella or the Vinaigre de Toilette from Diptyque, but it works just as well with cider vinegar. After your shampoo and conditioner, mix a few drops of vinegar in a bowl or large container of cold water and pour it on your scalp and hair. Do not rinse. It is going to dissolve all the chemical residues on your scalp and help keep it from getting greasy, and it also has some antibacterial benefits. Furthermore, it will give your hair incredible shine and lightness. It's an old recipe, but it does work!

You can also use a few spritzes of a vinegar solution at the roots to remove oil. Add five drops of apple cider vinegar to five ounces of water in a spray bottle, and this will replace your dry shampoo. Unlike dry shampoo, there's no residue, and the vinegar is a wonderful tonic for the scalp.

♥ Invest in a good hairbrush and take care of it

DAVID: A hairbrush is super important, and a lot of people stress and damage their hair using bad-quality or plastic brushes. For me, the best hairbrush in the world is made by Mason Pearson. They will last a long time, but you *must* look after them. You need to wash them with warm soapy water and then condition them. I condition all my brushes with a hair mask. I leave it on and then rinse really, really well. You *need* to rinse really well. And then your brush smells good, and it's good for your hair. I have some people who have said they haven't washed their brush in two years. You have to wash your brush at least once a month. Don't overbrush your hair, and finger-comb bits of it instead. Fingers are much softer than a comb!

♥ Supplements can improve your hair and scalp

DAVID: Brewer's yeast is a supplement that helps with regrowth and also hydrates the scalp. It is also great for the skin and the intestines; it is a wonderful regulator rich in probiotics. If you take it regularly, you will feel better, you won't get sick, and you will have beautiful hair. It also helps keep your hair clean longer, and is good for making your eyes sparkle!

LORRAINE: Hair has always been my weak point, and for years I have tried various treatments. I've had great results with brewer's yeast. If you take it regularly, you will feel better, and you will have beautiful hair that stays clean longer. I also take biotin; I apply one vial each of the French brands Biotine and Bépanthène and massage them into my scalp three times a week, and I take a Nourkrin capsule twice a day. In addition, Dexsil Pharma Organic Silicium has made a difference in my hair growth and has given me stronger nails as well as more mobility in my joints.

RAPHAËLLE'S HAIR-WASHING ROUTINE

My sister, Raphaëlle, has always had beautiful, enviably thick hair, and she takes such great care of it. She walked me through her regular regimen:

♥ Detangle hair with a quality brush before you get into the shower when you are going to shampoo it. The motion will help to move your hair's natural oils from the top to the bottom to protect your hair before you start shampooing it. You need to detangle before so that you do not have to do it after. Your hair is never as fragile as when it is wet!

♥ Use a very small amount of the shampoo best suited to your hair type on the scalp only, and emulsify with water. Don't rub the length of your hair with it. Gently massage your scalp with your fingertips (not your nails). And forget about foaming bubbles; many sulfate-free shampoos are foamless yet cleanse your hair and scalp better. It's just a question of getting used to it.

♥ After the extra-long shampoo rinse (recommended above by David and Christophe), gently wring the water from your hair and use a towel to half dry it when you're still in the shower. You don't want to dry it completely, but you also don't want to apply your conditioner to soaking wet hair. Imagine trying to apply your face cream on wet skin!

♥ Use your conditioner only on the length and the ends of your hair. Do not massage it into the scalp. If you have some time on your hands, let it penetrate for three to five minutes. Then comb and finish with an extra-long rinse again.

♥ After that step, gently squeeze the hair, but do not rub it dry. Whenever possible, try to have your hair dry naturally. (Although you don't want to be walking around with soaking hair!) Use a towel to remove as much water as possible. As your hair is very fragile when wet, do not rub or press your hair with a towel.

♥ If you are planning to use a hair dryer, use a heat setting no higher than medium, and keep the nozzle of the hair drier at a safe distance from your scalp.

♥ When your hair is fully dry, you can apply a pea-size amount of macadamia nut oil as a leave-in conditioner and shine agent. To do that, pour the oil onto your palm and rub both hands together until they are saturated, then gently run them through your hair. Finish by combing through the length and ends of your hair. I sometimes also use the macadamia oil on all the little hairs that tend to be difficult to tame on the top of my head. Warning: Do not ever put oil on your hair before using a hair dryer, as this can burn your hair.

♥ If you have long hair, it is much better to gather it all up before you go to bed so that it doesn't rub all night against the pillow. Try to do an easy braid or attach it in a loose bun on the top of your head.

♥ When you go on vacation in the sun, especially if you are going to swim in the sea or in a pool, be sure to rinse your hair as soon as you can after being in the water. Salt and chlorine are very damaging. That lovely blond surfers' look is great, but it does mean that your hair has become very dry.

ABOUT HAIR COLOR

Over time, hair loses its color. This is because the production of melanin, the pigmentation within hair follicles (which also determines your skin color), decreases as you get older. There is also a genetic component, which means you really don't have any control over when and how much your hair starts to go gray or white.

We're lucky that there are so many options for coloring your hair now, with healthier formulas with lower levels of peroxide, as well as conditioning elements that help lessen the effect of using chemicals on your hair. My advice is that you put off coloring your hair for as long as you can, because as I mentioned earlier, any kind of processing, even with more technologically advanced and gentler formulations, is always going to damage your hair. Once you do decide you're ready, then go for it and have some fun! Get the best possible advice from a really good colorist and treat this as if it were a makeup lesson. (One way to find an excellent colorist in your area is to simply ask someone who has the kind of color you like.)

Expert Hair Colorist Christophe Robin on Hair Color

If there is one man who understands the French attitude toward hair color, it's superstar colorist Christophe Robin. "French women aim for comfort and easy maintenance with their choice of hair color and are more attracted by a natural look, a look that reflects their personality," he says. "A brunette knows that it is quite difficult to transition to blond, as it's too much maintenance. It is true for clothes, nails, hair—the French woman makes comfort a priority. She would spend an hour for a mani-cure, but it has to last for at least a week."

Christophe began working as an apprentice in a hair salon in the town where he grew up when he was only fifteen, and he went to Paris at seventeen to work for Jean Louis David. One day he was given the opportunity, while on a shoot for L'Oréal, to cre-ate the color for supermodel Stephanie Seymour. It was such a hit that many other supermodels like Claudia Schiffer and Elle Macpherson hired him as well. His salon, dedicated solely to hair color, became a huge success. He explains: "At the time, you could find hair care for dry hair, but nothing for colored hair." No won-der Catherine Deneuve, with her iconic blond hair, became one of his regular clients and a friend. His recommendations will help you decide which color to choose and how to maintain your hair after it's been colored:

I think the most important thing is to stay comfortable with your age, to be in harmony with it. It's horrible when you are old and try to look young by choosing a platinum blond color, for example, or by apply-ing too much makeup. It just makes you look older. Accept your age and do not try to look young at any cost.

The best result is when you cannot tell if someone's hair is col-ored. Especially when you are covering the gray hair. Take a fifty-year-old brunette who wants to start covering the gray. If she chooses a brass or mahogany shade, it is not going to work because you can tell right away that the hair is colored. The most difficult thing is to maintain the natural look.

When you are young, it's okay to try crazy things; when you reach thirty, you must find the hair color that suits you. In your forties, stay true to your age with as much natural color as possible. If you like very dark hair, especially black, realize that black softens whatever is darker on the face. After sixty, many women think that they should try a very light or platinum blond—they think that is sexier and more luminous for someone their age, and it is just not true. When you get older, you get dark circles around the eyes, you get skin spots, the eyes lose some of their radiance, and if your hair is too blond, all you are going to see is the contrast, and all of these little defects are going to get highlighted instead of fading out. Look at Catherine Deneuve. She is in her seventies and her hair is a nuanced blond with darker lowlights, and this gives her a cool look, a younger look. If there are some nuances, especially dark lowlights, it is going to warm the complexion up and soften the face. They will erase the dark circles around the eyes and make the skin spots less visible.

Maintenance is also very important. To keep your hair coloration as long as possible, you have to take good care of it. My advice is to take good care of your hair as long as possible by applying a treatment once a week. That way, your color stays longer. In the United States, they use some techniques that we don't use at all in France. For example, they do a gloss treatment between colors. The gloss has a ten-volume oxidant component (*volume* is the professional name for what's added to bleach or color to trigger a reaction; twenty and thirty volume are what's typically used when you color your hair), a little ammonia, and color. It stays on the hair for ten to fifteen minutes only, but it is extra oxidation no matter what. It is a little bit like applying another layer of foundation on dry skin over and over again.

In France, we'd rather recommend taking the time to use a hair mask for an hour for results that will last about a week. For example, applying a hydrating mask once a week and sleeping with it on for an entire night is an ideal treatment, and it's as necessary as washing your hair with detergent-free shampoo. Would you wash your cashmere sweater or your silk blouse with a harsh detergent? Probably not. Same for the hair. It doesn't make sense.

When you are young and not yet going gray, you might still have a natural color that is a little dull, especially with ash-blond hair. It gives you a tired and not-so-healthy look. In this case, you need a light golden coloration, and you can use an all-natural product—for example, golden henna powder, which is 100 percent natural. You can mix some powder with your conditioner; leave it on for fifteen minutes, and rinse. It will give a boost to your complexion, and then you have not changed your hair color at all, just given it some easy highlights. Sometimes, if your hair is a little flat and lacks volume, you can get some highlights around the face.

Be Careful Before You Color Your Hair!

If you've ever bought a box of hair color to use at home, you know that the instructions always tell you to do a patch test first. That means you mix a tiny bit of color and apply it to your inner arm, wait for at least twenty-four to forty-eight hours, and then see if you have any kind of reaction. Most people ignore this step, but it's actually very important. Allergic reactions to the ingredients in hair color are rare, but they can be very harmful to your health.

How do I know this? Because it turned out that my mother was allergic to the toluene-2,5-diamine (a solvent often found in gasoline!) in the hair color product she used, and it had been affecting her for a long time. She had been coloring her hair for years, and only after a certain amount of this chemical had built up in her body did she begin to react to it. She felt incredible fatigue on a regular basis, and it is only thanks to a blood analysis that she was able to understand what was causing the problem. She was stunned.

Fortunately, once she stopped using that particular brand of color, her symptoms disappeared, and now she only uses organic products that are not as strong yet still do a great job covering any gray.

Bottom line: Read the instructions carefully and *always* do a patch test. If you have a reaction, do *not* use that color. Be aware that if you use peroxide on your hair, it is going to damage it, and you might see some hair loss. Consult a dermatologist if symptoms get worse or if you suddenly react to color (or any hair products) that have never bothered you before.

Your Scalp Needs a Good Detox Treatment

One of the beauty experts I interviewed several years ago told me something that made a lot of sense. "You take care of the skin on your face, of course," he told me, "but your scalp is still skin, so why don't people think about taking care of their scalp? It needs as much care as the skin on your face or neck."

I didn't realize how true that was until Dr. Guedj diagnosed me with psoriasis. Christophe Robin told me why: "When you color your hair, chemicals get into your hair and scalp. Over time, you may become allergic or sensitive to these chemicals," he explained. "Another problem is the silicone found in shampoos and conditioners. Very often, women do not rinse their hair well enough. You really need to rinse your hair thoroughly, until your hair becomes almost crisp to the touch. Residues of silicone can stay on your hair and get into your scalp; this keeps the scalp from breathing correctly, which leads to hair loss. This is why it is so important to detoxify the scalp."

Many of my friends with oily scalps swear by Christophe Robin's Cleansing Purifying Scrub with Sea Salt that is designed for use on the scalp—it's great right after you get your hair colored, especially if you have a rather oily scalp.

OUR HAIRSTYLES AND WHAT EXPERT STYLISTS TAUGHT US

A woman who cuts her hair is about to change her life.
—COCO CHANEL

David Mallett makes every woman who comes into his salon feel and look wonderful. "The approach is universal when women come to see a hairdresser; they want to look and feel beautiful," he says. "The only difference is that in Paris, beauty is not the same as elsewhere. French beauty for me, Parisian beauty, is an understated beauty. Even though it is extremely studied, the look is quite natural. It is not artificial, it's not plastic, and it is still a highly constructed beauty that is developed around the self and it is very balanced, in my eyes. Like a French garden, like French food. It's rarely eccentric, it's never outside of what you would expect. I find that when French women are beautiful, they are *very* beautiful."

What can hamper this beauty? "Really greasy hair, very flat-ironed hair, or stiff hair that doesn't move," he adds. "I like natural hair, I like shine, I like hair that smells good, I like hair that *moves* and seems happy. Real hair, that appeals to women *and* men, not just one or the other."

Wise words, as Coco Chanel, with her trademark sleek black bob, certainly knew the power of a good haircut.

RÉGINE: The Carita sisters opened their salon on the Faubourg Saint-Honoré in Paris in 1951, and they sold hair accessories in a small boutique there. Theirs was the first salon to sell wide black velvet headbands that created a very glamorous yet simple look—they were all about making women more beautiful and about creating sophisticated looks without going overboard. They added something undeniably sexy at a time when so many women were still sporting very stiff and elaborate styles.

About ten years later, I had my beautiful long hair cut short, as that style was becoming quite fashionable at the time. When I came back home after getting it cut, my husband was furious, especially because, as it turned out, we had to go to a black-tie event that very night. So I ran to the Carita salon, and the lovely Maria Carita used a fake hair ponytail to create a chignon that looked just like my own hair. It was so elegant, but to this day I still do not know how she attached that extension onto my hair that had been cut so short.

The Carita sisters taught me how to create incredible hairstyles thanks to what we call in French a *postiche,* or hairpiece. Women in France today are less into *grande coiffure* and *chignons* (buns); they all want blow-outs and avoid updos. But if one day you want to create a fabulous effect, adding a *postiche* will instantly transform your look.

LORRAINE: Most French women like their hair to be stylish but look effortless and not "done." We tend to favor a natural style, and if it is not perfect, even better! Sometimes the hairstyle is nearly a "just-out-of-bed" look that Bardot did so perfectly. (Not typical bed head—the "just-out-of-bed" is the kind of bed that has your lover in it!) We work to enhance what we have even if it is not something that is easy to tame or a particularly ravishing color we wish we had but we know wouldn't suit us. French women are not looking for volume but a stylish haircut that gives hair movement to make it a little sexy, with a look that is soft and subdued.

For years, my favorite place for hair was Carita. The Carita sisters' nephew, Christophe, was so talented. He knew how to give you the perfect length and the perfect volume for your face. When I was in my twenties and thirties, the Carita salon was packed on Saturdays. From Catherine Deneuve to the most famous socialites of Paris, we all had to wait to get our hair done, but we knew it was worth it. One day, this very well-known and elegant woman begged me to let her take my spot, as she was hosting a big ball in her home located on the Île Saint-Louis that same night, and she was desperate not to be late! There were still many big parties in Paris during those years. Women would appear with hairstyles that were elaborate and playful at the same time.

As for me, I have learned an infallible trick that has saved me from countless bad hair days when I'm rushing out of the apartment yet still want to look sophisticated and chic: I use an elastic hairband that makes me look as if my own hair has been braided. You simply put one on as you would a regular headband. Also, good-quality hair elastics are important so that you can wear them all day without damaging your hair.

These little tricks are ideal for me because while there are some women who love to change colors, hairstyles, and haircuts regularly, there are also those like me who are not adventurous with their hair and are happy to keep the same look for months and months (if not years!). I definitely belong to that second category. I think the most fun hair experience I ever had was with one of my best friends, who is Korean. She has very thick, straight hair and wanted to get a light perm for a wavier hairstyle. She took me to Koreatown in New York City, and we had so much fun waiting together with all these rollers and clips in our hair. It was unique to go there with her, as she could easily converse in Korean with the hairstylists, and I loved watching her explain exactly what she wanted, pointing to photographs in some of the professional-salon magazines and making sure the stylists were on the same page. Luckily for me, she was able to tell them that all I wanted was the lightest hint of a wave, as subtle as possible. I would never have risked it on my own!

Expert Hairstylist David Mallett on Hair and Beauty

David Mallett, as you've read already, is one of the most celebrated hairstylists in France and has worked with countless actresses, models, and celebrities, such as Kate Winslet, Andie MacDowell, Charlotte Rampling, Diane Kruger, Isabelle Adjani, Julianne Moore, Marion Cotillard, Naomi Campbell, Penélope Cruz, and Sharon Stone. He's created some of the most iconic images in fashion advertising and editorial in the past two decades with the world's most influential photographers.

Walking into David's hair studio immediately puts all of his clients at ease—one of the first things you see is an enormous stuffed ostrich. His environment is superchic and cozy, with tremendous flair. He doesn't just have hair salon–type mirrors that are lit with bulbs all the way around—he has a Marie Antoinette mirror with moldings all around it! And that is where he works his magic. As the master describes in his own words . . .

I always think that overdoing it is a common mistake that women make; overcoloring, overcutting, overstyling. Even if it is complicated to achieve, your hairstyle has to look easy and effortless. And I find that kind of *beauté négligée* really important. None of my clients are neglected in any sense at all, but I really like the results to look *easy*. Like you haven't made an effort even if, of course, you have! And that's really important for me—that things look effortless even if they are not. In the result, not in the way you get there.

This effortlessness needs to be something where your hairdresser educates you so that you can achieve it at home, so you can look just as good on Sunday morning as you do on Friday night. It's about beauty being involved in your life every day.

French Hairstyles You Can Do at Home

Renowned hairstylist Frédéric Fekkai has become one of the most successful hair entrepreneurs in America with his superchic hair salons and luxe hair-care products. He has recently launched a collection of natural beauty and home products from Aix-en-Provence, and he instructed me in the art of inimitable French styles you can easily do yourself.

The Perfect Chic Yet Casual Style Is the High or Low Ponytail

- After brushing your hair, spray your hairbrush with a smooth and shiny hair spray.
- Next, brush your hair back and create a ponytail, secured with one loop only of an elastic hair band.

- ♥ Spray it again with hair spray from the roots to the end of the ponytail.
- ♥ Secure the ponytail at the level height desired with tight loops.

The Sophisticated French Twist

- ♥ Part your hair on the side.
- ♥ Spray your hairbrush with a smooth and slightly shiny hair spray.
- ♥ Brush your hair back and make a ponytail.

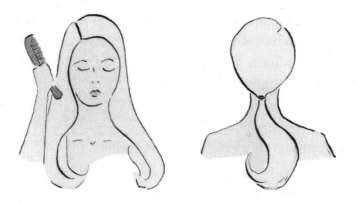

- ♥ Twist your ponytail, roll it up, and pin it in an oblong shape like a banana.

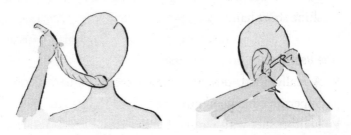

♥ Secure the ponytail with a large hairpin, and place smaller hairpins to hold the twist in place.

♥ Softly brush your hair and use a fine hair spray to finish.

To Blow Out Your Hair

♥ Apply a small amount of a volumizing mousse or spray at the roots.

♥ Pre-dry your hair upside down, focusing at the roots.

♥ Flip your hair back up, and use a round brush; the size of your brush should be according to your length (e.g., short hair/small brush) to dry your hair with the nozzle of a blow dryer.

♥ Always use a nozzle on your dryer, as this accurately directs the hot air.

♥ Use a downward motion, from the scalp to the ends, so you don't overheat or damage the cuticle of the hair.

To Add Volume to Your Hair

♥ Always use a volume spray or mousse at roots.

♥ Blow-dry your hair upside down before styling it.

For Short Hair

♥ I love to use either styling gel or pomade to style and shine short hair.

The Best Tools

♥ A really good, powerful blow dryer. The new Dyson Supersonic is a good one.

♥ Hairbrushes with natural bristles.

- ♥ I am not particularly a fan of flat irons, but ceramic ones are best.
- ♥ Same for curling irons.

Our Favorite Hair Products
For Hair Care and for Styling

Jeunesse: Shampoos from Klorane, Kérastase, John Masters Organics, and Captain Blankenship.

Try a dry shampoo such as the one from Klorane. Use only occasionally, as the more layers build up, the harder it is for your scalp to breathe.

For styling, my go-to products are a French braid–band synthetic hairpiece as well as Grab & Go Ponytail Holders by L.Erickson, which are soft and do not break the hair fiber.

Plénitude: Rahua, Macadamia Natural Oil Rejuvenating Shampoo, David Mallett, Leonor Greyl, and Christophe Robin. I recommend the CHI hair dryer as well as the new Dyson Supersonic hair dryer.

To touch up roots: Color Wow Root Cover Up is a genius mineral powder that can tide you over after a missed appointment.

Maturité: René Furterer and Phyto for both their shampoos and masks.

For All Ages:

These are our favorite tried-and-true products that will work whether you are twenty-five or eighty-five!

- ♥ Christophe Robin's Regenerating Mask with Rare Prickly Pear Seed Oil.

♥ Leonor Greyl Masque Fleurs de Jasmin.

♥ The one and only Mason Pearson hairbrush that is worth its price, as you will keep it forever. Wash your hairbrush regularly and this will prolong its life.

♥ Elnett hair spray. In the family, we still have not found a product to replace this one.

HAIR HEALTH PRIMER

Dr. Barbara Guedj is famous to those in the know in Paris as *the* hair dermatologist, and she is their first stop when any problems (like mine!) occur. This is her advice:

I am a dermatologist, so I treat skin, nail, and hair problems. When it comes to hair health, brittle hair, hair loss, the appearance of the hair in general—you have to consult a dermatologist, not a hairstylist. Because of new trends and fashion, hairdressers tend to damage hair, especially with Brazilian blow-outs or any new straightening technique that breaks the DNA of the hair. Sure, it looks great at first—but the hair is completely damaged afterward. You have to be very careful.

For brushing and combing, you can never be harsh with your hair, so the softer, the better. For *maturité*, you should use your fingers instead of a brush and brush your hair only once a week. Use a wide-tooth comb in order not to pull the hair. Do *not* blow-dry your hair if you start losing it. Air-dry it as much as possible.

Most of my patients come with concerns about hair loss. My first step is to check the thyroid, no matter how old the patient. When the thyroid gland doesn't function properly—whether in hyperthyroid mode (with overproduction of the thyroid hormones) or hypothyroid mode (with underproduction of the thyroid hormones)—it leads to hair loss. This requires medical treatment from a dermatologist or an endocrinologist. Do *not* go to a hair institute who will sell you extensions or a bogus miracle cream that costs a fortune and doesn't work.

How you style your hair can lead to hair loss, too. There can be cultural factors, with tight braids being the norm for women in some countries, but these are very bad for the hair and lead to hair loss. With frontal braids, chances are that your hairline will recede over time.

These days, it's all about hair extensions. Recently a top model came in, and she admitted that she was totally addicted to hair extensions. I had to tell her that the only way to fix the problem was to cut her hair very short because there was nothing I could do until she stopped using them. The extra weight of the extensions was leading to irreversible hair loss, and she had bald spots all over her head. Some hairdressers refuse to do straightening and extensions, and they recommend a really good haircut instead. So be cautious of the new trends. They could work for one evening or a party, but it's wiser to use a wig or a hairpiece if you really want a different look.

Finally, remember that food and stress are important factors. Women feel that they have to be skinny, but when you lose a lot of weight you may start losing your hair, too. You cannot be excessive or extreme with weight-loss diets. Luckily, you can take vitamins B1, B6, B12, as well as zinc and iron, which help fix this problem. And as we all know, eating a lot of fruits and vegetables is not only good for your overall health but also for your hair. Any food with high levels of vitamin C, such as citrus, will improve hair health.

Yes, There Is Such a Thing as a Hair Biologist!

Bruno Bernard is one of a handful of world experts in the biology of hair, and he has been studying it for over three decades. I found what he had to say completely fascinating, especially as it's so easy to take our hair for granted and not care for it properly. Here's what he told me:

The hair follicle is one of the most complex organs in the human body. A single hair follicle has about fifteen different types of cells, which are distributed in five different compartments.

Our scalps have about 150,000 hair follicles that are asynchronous; each follicle has an independent cycle, and this cycle is somewhat chaotic. Hair growth is not on a fixed time. It can vary from one follicle to the next and even for a single follicle itself. This behavior is very important, as it allows us to always have hair on our heads!

Many people complain about hair loss when the real problem is, in fact, *brittle* hair, especially in India, where many women have very long hair. Hair that is overtreated, especially if it is very long, becomes fragile.

Over time, hair gets damaged first at the cuticle, then at the roots, and then at the ends, which often split.

Weekly blow-drying is bad for the hair, and so is coloring if it happens too often. Although men tend to have more hair loss due to hormones, women's hair is almost always much more damaged because of all these treatments.

Nutrition is very important, too, as it is fundamental for hair growth. If you don't have enough arginine, an amino acid produced by your adrenal glands in limited quantities, you should ensure normal levels by eating arginine-rich foods, such as poultry, dairy, or soybeans. But it is still very hard to know which foods will have the strongest effect on hair strength.

Today we have treatments adapted for each level of damage. I often advise hairdressers to measure hair in *time* length rather than in hair length itself. As your hair grows about four-tenths of an inch per month, on average, if your hair is thirty-six months old, for example, lots of things will have happened to it during that time.

Don't believe the hype about "all-natural" hair-care products. An ingredient being natural doesn't mean that it will be less dangerous than something synthetic. The most violent poisons and potent allergens are natural—such as snake venom and tree pollen! Some synthetic ingredients happen to be better and less harmful than some natural ingredients. There is no one rule for all. Use common sense and be aware of your own needs—what works for someone else might not be good for you.

Part Five

Life et les Bonnes Habitudes

Chapter 9

The Four Pillars of French Wellness

As life is an art in France, so woman is an artist.

—EDITH WHARTON

I never thought I would live in America—I always thought I would end up somewhere between London or Barcelona, cities I knew and loved. But when I got engaged to a New Yorker and moved to the Big Apple with him, it was the most exciting time for me. I still remember how impressed I was that Indian summer, eleven years ago, by all these women in the city with their slick gym outfits, a coffee or latte in their large paper cups, and an energy you would just never see in the streets of Paris at eight a.m! On weekends while taking a walk with my then fiancé, I bumped into some New York friends heading to yoga, with their trendy yoga-mat bags slung across their backs and their hair pulled back in high ponytails. I was still into classical dance and swimming, while everybody I was meeting was raving about the latest fitness trend at their gym or workout studio. As a French woman, I had not grown up with the American fitness culture; at school we hardly ever did more than two hours of sports a week, and we did not have any sports facilities in most schools or colleges. To be healthy, we had to eat healthy and sleep well—and yes, of course, add a little exercise here and there.

But New York's energy became so contagious that I quickly adopted the fast-paced lifestyle of the city. I have tried the most *au courant* barre class and all sorts of new trends, and I now stick to a great balance of cardio-dance, Pilates, yoga, and a little swimming when I can. But I still cannot head to the office in my sneakers or drop my children at school while wearing my fitness clothing—a French woman would *never*! (If she's doing the school run, for example, she'll throw on a trench coat—it hides a multitude of fashion sins and always looks chic.) My workout gear is always folded as much as possible and hidden at the bottom of my work tote bag.

I've come to realize the French have a lot to learn, especially for children, in terms of the great benefits of sports and exercise at school. The positive energy it creates truly helps us feel better, learn better, and work better. But I've also learned that a healthy lifestyle is not only about running to the gym every day—it is a regular process to add to our daily routine, from the moment we wake up to the moment we go to bed.

You'll see what I mean in this chapter, which covers the four pillars of French wellness: eating smart, posture and breathing, exercise, and sleep *à la française*.

PILLAR #1: FOOD—BACK TO BASICS

I spent most of my childhood summers with my family in Brittany, the northwest province of France located on the Atlantic Ocean. It was very rustic there, with salty sea breezes constantly blowing, making the air clean and fresh. Practically every day, we'd run with our nets down to the beach with our cousins, especially at low tide, and the seafood was so abundant that we could literally pick up dozens and dozens of crabs and shrimp. These shrimp were tiny, and all we had to do was pull off the head and skin and they were ready to eat. Our grandparents would go to the local *boulangerie* in the morning for enormous loaves of fresh bread, and we'd make toast with fresh salted butter and pile all the briny shrimp on top. I'd be so proud of my delicious shrimp, but far too often, just as I was about to eat it, one of my older cousins would sneak into the kitchen and steal it! Those sunny summers taught me all about the wonders of eating fresh and eating local.

Back in Paris for the school year, we would always look forward to snack time. This was at school, where we would be given a small piece of a freshly baked baguette along with a few squares of dark (*never* milk!) chocolate to make our own *pain au chocolat*. We'd happily devour it, the slightly bitter chocolate melting into the warm bread, and it would tide us over until dinnertime. We didn't realize that dark chocolate is loaded with antioxidants and other micronutrients—we were just hungry and loved our snack. It also took me many years to realize that I rarely ate any other sugar during the day, except perhaps for a bit of jam or honey on my baguette for breakfast. As a result, I never developed the sweet tooth that I find so alarming in my children's classmates. If you grow up eating sweets all the time—or seeing them as a treat rather than just a very small part of your daily diet—your palate becomes used to needing sugar, and it becomes very hard to disengage from what you're craving.

In our Parisian neighborhood, the only way to shop was at the many small food stores selling only one kind of item—a fishmonger would never sell meat, and the butcher would never sell fish; we'd go to the *fromagerie* for cheeses and fresh milk and butter, and the greengrocer for fruits and vegetables. We knew what we were buying because it was fresh, and our local shops took great pride in purchasing top-quality foods. So when I moved to New York, walking into Whole Foods in Union Square and seeing what was gorgeously arranged on three enormous floors was definitely a shock. I was entranced by the choices but also bewilderingly overwhelmed, as most Europeans are, especially by the rows and rows of food in boxes or in the freezers. If my mother did buy something prepackaged, it rarely had more than three ingredients—which is how I choose my chocolate. When you read the list of ingredients, they should be items that your grandmother would have known in her time. If you have difficulty pronouncing any of the ingredients from the list, especially if they are long strings of chemicals, either research what they are or choose something you know is good for you!

We ate simply, because if your food is very fresh, it needs little adornment other than seasoning. Our meals were well balanced, with small portions of protein and much larger portions of vegetables and whole grains. We also followed the wonderful French habit of ending the meal on a savory, not sweet, note—with a salad, dressed in a vinaigrette made from delicious olive oil, a splash of red wine vinegar, and a bit of pungent Dijon mustard. Sometimes, we had a cup of relaxing chamomile tea. Rarely did we feel the need for a snack before bed, either.

I didn't realize at the time how common sense defined how we ate. We ate what is now called the Mediterranean diet—rich in vegetables and fruit, whole grains, olive oil, and small amounts of animal protein. When you eat this way, you automatically reap the health benefits of satisfying food that is high in fiber and taste, yet low in sugar. Ironically, this is how Americans used to eat—before the introduction of fast food and packaged foods in the 1950s and 1960s—when far fewer people were overweight and sedentary, and obesity-related illnesses such as type 2 diabetes were a rarity.

I must add that not everything I was taught about nutrition when I was growing up was always true. My mother would tell me that cherries were so full of sugar that they were bad for us, because she'd been told they were, and that avocados weren't good for you because they were all fat, but we didn't know that there is an important difference between good polyunsaturated fats like the kind in avocados and the bad saturated fats like the kind in marbled meat or shortening. (Which is why I now eat at least an avocado a day and don't think twice about its fat content!) We also ate a lot of red meat all the time, and even though it was grass-fed French meat and the portions were far smaller than what is typically served in America, it's still better to have a lot of fish or vegetarian meals, too.

One thing that was very true for us, though, was that our children ate what the grown-ups ate. No kiddie menus exist for French children, so the first time I went with my children to an American friend's home for a holiday party, I was very surprised to see a separate table with a heaping plate of chicken nuggets—a food item that French parents would never allow their children to eat. Over on the side was a small plate of carrot sticks, but who would want to eat that when there was another table laden with

Christmas cookies and other sweet treats? Not me! Steam the carrots, please, or put them in a pot with a little bit of butter, or at least roast them. For a once-in-a-while treat, chicken nuggets or cupcakes are fine, of course, but I decided to teach my children to make reasonable choices.

One thing I did learn from the Italians (not the French!) after traveling often to Italy was to treat cheese more like a condiment than a large part of your meal. This was hard for me because I love cheese, but once I saw how the Italians grated their parmesan from an enormous wheel onto their pasta, with perhaps no more than a teaspoon of cheese, I realized that a small amount gave just the right touch of piquant flavor. When your food is very flavorful, you do eat less of it, because your taste buds quickly become satiated.

I am very glad these eating habits were instilled in me during my childhood, because I learned to cook basic yet delicious meals using fresh food. I enjoy cooking as long as it does not take the whole afternoon! I like to make my meals in the shortest time possible, so what I do is turn on the French channels streaming on my computer so I can listen to the news from home. That makes me happy and also makes the food prep seem less tedious.

There are several other important aspects of how we eat:

Please Sit Down at the Table

If you've ever seen French movies, they usually have scenes set around the table, often leaving you wanting to run right into the closest French café in your neighborhood afterward because everything just looked so good! Eating *en famille* is a national tradition. My parents would have dinner with *their* parents growing up, and I did the same as a child. Today I am perpetuating this well-ingrained habit of making sure we have most evenings together as a family.

I'm sure you already know about this concept, especially if you've been to France, and I also know how hard it can be to have regular mealtimes when you are juggling many other obligations. But I believe it is vitally important to sit down as a family and eat together whenever possible. My husband, children, and I usually eat *early*. We use this precious hour to talk to the children about their day at school and to share what happened to us at work. All cell phones are left in another room. We eat slowly and savor our food, which is better for your digestion. This leisurely approach to mealtime, even if there are pressing tasks to attend to afterward, is teaching our children not only the importance of taking the time to eat without rushing but to look forward to our time together. I can see my children and husband visibly relaxing and unwinding from the time they sat down to the time when the meal is over. And if you are on your own, it is just as important to keep regular hours, to eat simple yet fresh and delicious food, to set your table, and sit down to eat.

Supersized Is for Bottles of Body Lotion, Not Food!

This won't come as news to you, I am sure, but it *is* true that some restaurants in certain countries (like America) offer very large portion sizes. And this can create a little frustration when customers go to French restaurants and are given much smaller sizes than they are used to. Often, my American friends tease me about this and tell me that the French are just "being snobs," but small portions are how the French eat.

As for me, it took quite a while to adjust to meals being supersized in America. I don't like the idea of wasting food; I tend to order smaller portions. I mostly make vegetarian choices, too, because I don't want to eat too much meat.

Les Faux Amis, or High-Calorie Drinks Are Fake Friends

Changing eating habits is difficult for anyone, but one thing that is much easier to control is what you drink—or rather, what you *don't* drink—during the day. While you are very unlikely to see a French woman eating a bagel with cream cheese, because we definitely prefer a fresh croissant when we find them, you are equally unlikely to see a French woman in a local coffee shop ordering an extra-large café latte or iced coffee drink, or a super-sweetened iced tea. We will go to a café for a quick little espresso, often drunk at a counter while standing up, or make a small cup at the office.

Drinking espresso is a wonderful habit I picked up in Italy, and now, for me, it's the perfect amount of coffee. When you make filter or drip coffee, you're passing water through the grounds and you can end up with way too much caffeine. (A small espresso, which is more like a shot and is usually no more than one ounce of liquid, has from 40 to 75 mg of caffeine, while an eight-ounce cup of regular coffee has anywhere from 80 to 185; a twenty-ounce Starbucks Blonde Roast Venti has a whopping 475 mg, which you would only need if you have to stay awake for a big project!) A small espresso has 1–3 calories, whereas a latte with sugar can have hundreds. It is incredibly easy to forget how many calories are in drinks.

In most homes in France, you grow up with water as your beverage; my parents might have had a glass of wine with lunch or dinner, and probably an espresso at the end of a meal, but the rest of the time it was just water. We never had soda when I was little, and we rarely drank juice, either. Since French parents would not provide apple or other juices to their children, their little ones never developed a taste for sweet drinks. We are the ones responsible for feeding our children, so if we do not offer these sweet drinks at home, they won't expect them and crave them, and it won't become a habit that can be very hard to undo.

We've always had bottles of mineral water readily accessible, which is a particularly French/European habit, as there are a great variety of waters available, sourced from natural mineral springs in France and other countries and each with a unique taste depending on its mineral content. My mother was particularly fond of Châteldon and La Salvetat; my sister loved Evian and Volvic. I believe that the palates of many French people, without them ever necessarily realizing it, become accustomed to specific brands, and we develop certain taste buds for them. Some other well-known brands include Thonon, Hépar (good for the liver and used also when children have stomach bugs), Cristaline, Vichy Célestins, and Saint-Yorre. And there's also our trusted ally during diets: the mineral water Contrex. This water has a peculiar taste due to its high levels of calcium and magnesium. I can still sing the Contrex jingle from the ads that I heard on TV when I was little!

Although I was taught the good habit of drinking pure, mineralized spring water, no one carried bottled water around or worried about how much water they were drinking during the day. I provide myself with more than enough hydration from eating fruit and vegetables with a high water content. Not only are they low in calories, but they are super-hydrating and delicious.

The best hydrators for me are cucumbers, pomegranates, avocados, apricots, mangoes, broccoli, and spinach.

We Watch Our Weight

A journalist named Didier Raoult recently wrote an article for the weekly French magazine *Le Point* about the particularity of French eating habits. Why, he wondered, is France falling less quickly into obesity than other countries around the world? French (and Italian) women have been incredibly good at maintaining their weight, and Raoult explained it from an interesting historical point—namely, that French stylishness and *coquetterie* have been admired and imitated for centuries. The first women to have spent most of their lives dieting to keep a youthful silhouette were French women.

Raoult mentions that studies have also shown that regular attention paid to your appearance is a positive factor for improving your health. French women who like to think of themselves as having an ineffable elegance consider a certain figure to be an essential part of that. Not a bone-thin silhouette or a weight that is maintained by a super-restrictive diet devoid of pleasure (like dark chocolate!), but one that obliges them to be aware of what and how much they eat, and not to fall into a total *laisser aller.* The effect, obviously, of healthy eating over a lifetime cannot be denied—just as those who start taking care of their skin and protecting it from the sun when they are young have a much smoother and less wrinkled face than those who are perpetual sun worshippers. A sensible weight and an elegant silhouette are hallmarks not only of elegance but of a determination to keep weight-induced medical conditions like type 2 diabetes and high blood pressure at bay.

Dr. Georges Mouton on the Impact of Food on Our Skin

The best skin comes from within—and that means extra-healthy nourishment. Nutritionist and functional medicine expert Dr. Georges Mouton shared his practical advice about foods that are good for your complexion:

It is important to eat foods that are what we call nutrient-dense, as they give you the most nutrients for the fewest calories. Vegetables, fruits, whole grains, seafood, eggs, beans and peas, unsalted nuts and seeds, fat-free and low-fat dairy products, and lean meats and poultry are all nutrient-dense. In addition, they all have little or no saturated fat, sodium, or added sugars. This also means eating fresh food, not packaged or processed, as no foods are more nutrient-dense than whole, organically grown foods.

Eating red meat once a week, not more, has some benefits, as it contains iron, zinc, and vitamin B12, all of which I find to be fundamental. (People who don't eat red meat should undergo an analysis to see if they are lacking in any of these three essential micronutrients; if so, they should consider introducing some red meat to their diets.) As far as the protein content is concerned, an alternative could be white meat and fish.

Other key ingredients for healthy skin include vitamin E (almonds), vitamin D (fish), vitamin C (citrus fruit), B vitamins (green leafy vegetables, eggs, corn, nuts, poultry), vitamin A (fish oils), lycopene (tomatoes), lutein (carrots), coenzyme Q10 (red meat, oily fish), zinc (oysters), and selenium (Brazil nuts).

As far as sugar is concerned, there is no such thing as good sugar. There is no escaping this fact. I focus on the fructose aspect, knowing that sugar is usually half glucose, half fructose. You should eat no more than an ounce or so (twenty-eight grams) of fructose a day, unless you are very active. Bear in mind that the fructose found in fruits is much healthier than high-fructose corn syrup or other added sugars. And don't be fooled by packaging. For example, fruit juice that says "No added sugar" may have no sucrose but will be full of fructose. Look for the sugar grams listed on the food label.

The Best Foods for Improving Your Circulation

Here is a list of tips from Orthopédie Meyrignac's Caroline Meyrignac for healthy blood and good circulation. This will, of course, help with cell growth and organ function. Poor circulation, on the other hand, leaves you looking uneven and blotchy.

- Soft fruits and berries (black currants, strawberries, gooseberries).
- Avocado, eggs, nuts, hazelnuts, almonds.
- Vegetables: cabbage, carrot, sweet potato, bell pepper, broccoli, pumpkin, spinach.
- Pungent vegetables like onions and garlic.
- Poultry, white meat, fish, or seafood; minimal amounts of red meat.
- Foods without any added sugar.
- Avoid processed and packaged foods.
- Cook your food in the oven, on a grill, or steamed, and try to add fats afterward (vegetable oils, preferably).
- Do not oversalt your food. If you are eating with salt, be sure to use salt that is well iodized.
- You may drink one glass of red wine from time to time. Red (not white) wine is full of resveratrol, a potent antioxidant.

A Few Words About Smoking

LORRAINE: Once, when I was with Diana Vreeland, she asked me if I was engaged. I said, "No, not really!" She asked what my boyfriend did for a living, and I told her that he was working in the manufacturing of rolling papers for cigarettes. "Cigarettes?" she said. "Cigarettes? My dear, this will not do. Cigarettes are going to vanish. Tell him it's not a right business to be in."

Diana Vreeland was quite the visionary about fashion, and she also understood that smoking was on the way out. Although the number of smokers has drastically decreased in France, many still resist and either start smoking or keep on smoking even though they can't say they aren't aware of the health risks. This is why many Americans who've gone to Paris or other French cities over the years have returned home with one particularly indelible memory: how much the French still smoke.

When I was growing up, practically everyone smoked. You could barely find a café in which to sit down with your hot chocolate and a croissant without smoke wafting in your face. Women smoked, too, confessing that they usually started because they thought it would help them keep the weight off.

It is extremely difficult to stop smoking, but if you still like your cigarettes, please reconsider. You already know how terribly toxic they are. Your skin will thank you. Your body will thank you. And everyone around you will thank you!

PILLAR #2: STAND TALL—POSTURE
AND CORRECT BREATHING

Alignment is enlightenment.

—B. K. S. IYENGAR

I think you know by now that I love Brigitte Bardot; she is particularly inspiring to me in two of her movies: *Le Mépris* (*Contempt*, from 1963) and *La Vérité* (*The Truth*, from 1960).

In *Le Mépris*, there is one particular scene that takes place in Capri, Italy, at the famous Villa Malaparte, in which Bardot walks barefoot on those ochre-colored stones with the deep blue of the Mediterranean behind her. It isn't an ordinary walk—it's the walk of a dancer. She looks almost feline in the way she moves her feet, one in front of the other, with impeccable grace. And in *La Vérité*, there is an absolutely magnificent moment when Bardot's character, Dominique, wakes up, turns on some music, and starts to dance, naked, near her window. The arch of her feet and the way she moves are mesmerizing. Not just in their casual sexiness—but because her posture is so impeccable at that moment. She made me want to move in the same way. To stand tall and straight and move with grace.

Posture is a topic that is rarely discussed, and yet it is more important than ever, because in our digital world, where even toddlers are swiping their little fingers on their iPads, we are always looking down, not up. I'm not really joking when I say that the only people happy about this are chiropractors and physical therapists, because we are causing incalculable damage to our bodies when we walk with our heads down, staring at our phones or cradling them between our ears and shoulders. Or sitting at office desks for long periods, slouching and staring at a misaligned computer. No wonder our heads, necks, and backs are constantly aching!

When I was growing up, sitting with a straight back at the table was the rule, and remarks about our posture were definitely something that regularly came out of my parents' mouths. Especially during the teen years when our spines were unfortunately way too flexible, with nothing to push our hair back so that it wouldn't end up covering half of our faces. *"Tiens toi droite!"* (Sit up straight!) is what my parents (and my friends' parents!) told us again and again.

These constant reminders, of course, drove me crazy at the time, but I'm now so glad they nagged at me to stop slouching, as I understand how important it is to concentrate on your posture. Good posture not only has the immediate benefit of improving your breathing and strengthening your core muscles, but it is also a way to feel more confident; you present yourself to others in a better way. Nevertheless, it is still hard for me to remember to stand straight all the time.

The sooner you can instill the very necessary muscle memory that will keep your body properly aligned with good posture, the better. It's so important to be aware of your world and to present yourself to others with strength and body confidence. It will boost your enthusiasm and energy. You should always walk down the street focusing on the horizon, *not* your phone! That way, you keep your body in alignment. Pull your shoulders back. Tighten your abdominals. Move with power. Waiting for the light so you can cross the street? Use these precious seconds to realign your body and do all the things listed above. It will make it easier to hold that posture later that evening when you are at a cocktail party, gracefully and effortlessly weaving your way through the crowd and standing with confidence and power. Helena Rubinstein repeated like a mantra that beauty was nothing if the body wasn't maintained. More recent studies have found that posture has a direct impact on our mood and that slouching impacts our self-esteem and energy.

By working on your posture, you are telling everyone that you are at ease with the world in the best way you can. Keeping your shoulders open, with your neck long and extended, try to sit and keep your back straight. All these details actually transform you. Try it and see that it can really help you show the best of yourself!

Everyone Needs Good Posture, Mobility, and Flexibility

Austrian-born Lilian Arlen was a dancer and a physiotherapist who made it her life's work to help people improve their posture, mobility, and longevity. Béatrice Arapoglou, an ex-dancer from London Opera, trained with Lilian and worked with her for fifteen years before taking over her clientele. Their work merges the best of ballet and yoga, and you don't have to be a dancer to reap its rewards. Here are some words of wisdom Béatrice recently shared with me:

What's most important is to have strong spine flexibility and joint mobility. This has nothing to do with muscles, a flat belly, or wanting to get a hazelnut-shaped butt. People think that muscle work is everything, when it's not. Too much muscle development *impairs* mobility so you can't move properly. You need your muscles, of course, but *deep* muscles. In general, people work on *superficial* muscles, especially those who jog and run. They damage their vertebrae, hips, and breasts. It is so much better to walk!

Mixing up different kinds of exercise is better than doing the same thing every day, and exercising for twenty minutes a day is better than doing one hour three times a week.

Consider deep stretches that will tone and give length to your muscles. It is not difficult to stretch. You can do it at home—all you have to do is try to reach the ceiling with your arms up for two minutes at a time. Try to do this several times a day.

For *maturité* and women going through perimenopause or menopause, it is important to maintain bone health to postpone osteoporosis and other age-related factors. If you can't work with a trainer or exercise on your own, you can still stretch, move, go up and down stairs, and try not to gain weight, which adds a lot of stress to your joints.

If you start late, yoga is your best option. Hatha yoga is the best for movement. There is also tai chi. Swimming and walking are easily available to all.

Remember, a young body is a flexible body. If you want to stay young, you have to *move*. That is the key to well-being, even for older women. The result is that you move easily, gracefully, and it is a beautiful thing. If you see an old woman walking gracefully and easily, not only does she look beautiful, but she also looks *young*.

Setting Up an Ergonomically Correct Desk

Chiropractor Dr. Hagop Alajajian shared this information, which is important for your circulation and energy. No slouching at your desk, please! As for me, my favorite tool is a yoga block that I use at the office and place between my back and the back of the chair. It immediately helps me to remain straight.

Make sure that while sitting or standing, your head and shoulders are retracted backward, aligning your ears, shoulders, and hips in a straight line.

When using computers, the top of the monitor should be at or slightly below your eye level at approximately an arm's-length distance.

When sitting at your desk, once again your shoulders should be retracted backward, your lower back supported to prevent slouching, and your upper arms kept parallel to your body.

When using a keyboard, your elbows should be close to the side of your body, at a 90-degree angle as your hands rest in neutral position on the keyboard.

Keep your hips and knees at equal planes, bent at a 90-degree angle.

The use of an ergonomic desk, chair, and footrest can be used to assist you in staying in this position, if needed.

Getting up and stepping away from your desk frequently during long periods of work is something you always need to do.

Stretching and simple core exercises should be performed daily for proper maintenance and support.

The Importance of Proper Breathing

Breathing is something we also take for granted, but once you learn how to breathe properly, you will automatically feel better, be able to regulate your stress more quickly by focusing on your breathing, and get more energy because you're oxygenating your body in the way it needs.

In addition to his breathing techniques, licensed masseur-physiotherapist Christophe Marchesseau is also a proponent of therapeutic massage. Don't think of massage as a luxury or as a pampering. Regular massages, as he puts it, make you feel relaxed, readjusted, grounded and regenerated. Here is some of his advice on breathing:

My advice for women of all ages is to become aware of their breathing, and pay attention to the *exhale*. Most of the time and in our daily life, we are in a state of respiratory apnea. The lungs are filled up with air, like two helium balloons that would lift us up off the ground. We don't even think of emptying them—yet it is so important to *exhale*. In other words, to blow the air out. The inhale process is a reflex; you don't have to think about it because without it you will die! Exhaling properly is something you can definitely teach yourself.

The abdominal muscles are respiratory muscles, and they make your abdominal wall firmer. This exercise also has an effect on another major muscle as far as breathing is concerned: the diaphragm. The diaphragm is the massage therapist of your body and has an effect on your circulation. Working the diaphragm massages your belly area and helps with the relaxing of your abdomen, which, according to some studies, acts as a second brain. It's very easy to do this exercise in full awareness of the process at home and at any time:

1. Sit on the edge of a chair and make sure you are in a stable position.
2. Feel your seat bones in contact with the chair, straighten your back, stretch upward, and let your shoulders relax. Then, purse your lips together and steadily exhale through your nose for as long as you are able to, while maintaining the stretch. Try to visualize your belly button reaching the back of your spine. Force the exhale until you can feel your belly becoming harder.
3. You can do this as often as you like.

In order to achieve the best results, with proper breathing, the only secret is discipline on a daily basis. What at first can feel like a burden and a pain becomes a pleasant experience. The benefits are worth the effort!

PILLAR #3: THE EXERCISE AND
MOVEMENT YOU NEED

Going to summer camp in America was my first big experi-ence with how American girls my age exercised. No doubt about it, they were *much* more active! They did all kinds of sports and ran around and got sweaty and had fun. I was, of course, far behind in every discipline, and the worst for me was during my first year at camp, when I was considered such a weak swimmer that I was not allowed to do any water sports on my own. (Con-sidering that I loved to swim, this was totally humiliating!) I did not let that happen the next summer, but I was still the least ath-letic camper by far, having no idea how to play so many of the American sports that we would practice daily, like lacrosse, bas-ketball, baseball, and volleyball.

As adults, many French women prefer traditional exercises, such as stretching, yoga, and dance, and we ignore the latest gym trends. When we find a trainer or a class we like, we stick to it. As Béatrice said earlier in this chapter, we know that moving is living; what makes us look young is how well and how often we move.

So when I moved to New York, I was a bit astonished to see how many people were running in Central Park. I quickly grew to love going there, cycling with my husband and children, as I found it incredibly satisfying how you never feel alone there. There's always something going on. The energy and determina-tion are infectious!

I definitely consider myself much more of a New Yorker now, and I'm very active and walk everywhere, but like many French women I don't want to do the kinds of exercises that can quickly bulk you up and change your body into something that is a little less feminine for my taste.

My regular exercise routine is, as I mentioned earlier in this chapter, to do either cardio-dance, Pilates, yoga, or a thirty-minute swim once a week. I also like to go for bike rides in Central Park on weekends when weather permits. When I'm back in Paris, I walk, walk, walk, and of course I visit Béatrice and take one of her classes.

Exercise definitely makes you feel great, even if it is not an intensive class. People talk about becoming addicted to their regular runs or classes or workouts at the gym, and I totally understand why. Your body just knows that you are doing something good for it and naturally keeps asking for more. Most of my French friends now wouldn't dream of missing their regular exercise routines, and they are much more likely to have their children practice sports outside of school hours. French schools still have very few weekly sports, and few of them even have gyms or locker rooms in the building. From first to twelfth grade, I only had two hours of gym class every *week*. With the time it took to get changed, the twenty minutes it took walking to the playing field, and the twenty minutes to walk back to school, we would barely even have forty-five minutes of proper exercise each week. And when the weather was very rainy and horrible—as it often is in Paris—we wouldn't go outside at all!

Vitalité Is Key

One topic I often discuss with my mother and grandmother is how they feel physically as they grow older. Something they have told me is that it is much easier to grow older with grace and serenity if you have prepared for it emotionally *and* physically. For my mother, the key word is *vitalité*. This is what you want to keep as you get older.

So my mother follows a regular routine of Pilates and stretching, and she adds more to her routine when she goes on vacation. She was always a trendsetter in our family, and I remember her buying equipment many years ago for aquatic gymnastics, where you do your workout in a pool. She later started attending aqua-bike classes when this kind of in-pool exercising was not very well known yet. She surprised the whole family a few years ago when she proudly showed off an incredible mask she'd just gotten—it was a mask and snorkel combined in one piece, making her look like an alien when she put it on, but was incredibly practical when it came to snorkeling.

For Lorraine and Régine, getting older does not mean that they suddenly stop all their good habits. *Au contraire!* As you go from your sixties into your seventies, even for those who are in excellent health, it gets harder to maintain a normal weight. Circulation and metabolism slow down, and that makes energy levels decline, too. That means you don't feel like much activity—but it is so important to force yourself to *move*. To get up, sit down, go get something, and then repeat it all over again.

This is where the vital concept of *discipline* comes in, something I have been taught well by my uncle Guy as well as by my grandmother, as I mentioned earlier in the book.

RÉGINE: I recently recalled something my own mother would tell me all the time when she was very old: "The bed is a woman's worst enemy at my age!" Because the older you get, the more often you want to spend time in bed and the less you want to move. And you have to fight that!

So I push myself to take long walks and to do physical activities outside the house every day. We must keep good habits and mental equilibrium. It's a mental discipline. And the older we get, the more good habits we need to keep and thus, the stronger our routine must be.

I am in awe of my grandmother. I know it can be very difficult for her to get out and move on a gloomy and damp day when all you want to do is stay indoors in a lovely warm room with a good book—but she still does it. I love that she is using her cell phone to track her daily activities, and I love it even more when she tells me that she reached five thousand steps for the day. I often don't walk that much!

The Best Exercise to Improve Your Circulation

As we get older, our circulation often becomes more sluggish, which is why regular exercise is so important for your cardiovascular system. Getting the heart pumping and blood flowing is not just great for making your cheeks rosy and flushed but also for improving your general state of well-being. It's especially important if you spend a lot of hours sitting at a desk, as the more sedentary you are, the more the blood stagnates in your legs, leaving you at a higher risk for varicose veins and other issues. So get moving! This is what Caroline Meyrignac recommends:

Walking, at least one to two miles per day, preferably at a brisk pace, is ideal. Swimming or aqua-gym: Movements in the water (such as kicking or cycling) are particularly beneficial, as the pressure of the water on the veins helps them, and the buoyancy of the water takes pressure off your joints. Cycling is also great, outdoors or indoors. At the gym: If it is a soft kind of exercise, it will help with the muscle maintenance of the entire body. Jogging and running: Caution! If you want to jog, make sure you are wearing the right kind of shoes—look for those with a high level of shock absorption—and try to run on softer ground. Hard asphalt is very tough on your veins, feet, and legs.

If you have problems with your circulation, avoid sports that involve a lot of high impact, jumping, straining, or hitting, such as rugby, soccer, football, tennis, boxing, or sprinting.

PILLAR #4: *DORMEZ-VOUS?*

From my childhood to this day, it was always key for me to keep my bedroom as dark as possible. It is a habit I have kept through the years, making sure I always have thick curtains or blackout shades. This is something I feel I can control, while it is not always easy to control the noise when you live in a big city—whether it comes from inside the apartment (the pipes clanking in the winter when the heating goes on) or outside (the endless streams of traffic; the sirens just when you are about to conk out).

Although Paris is not a quiet city, it is not as loud as New York. I miss the feeling of near silence at night that I had in our Paris apartment when I was growing up and the true silence you get in the countryside. I miss sleeping with windows wide open in the warm summer nights (few apartments have air-conditioning in Paris, as it is rarely needed!). And although you would occasionally hear some locals who were a little too happy from their night out at the local café singing in the streets on the weekends, or Vespas with their annoying whine suddenly tearing through the silence of the Parisian night, otherwise the silence was deep and restful.

In terms of ambiance, when I was growing up there was really no such thing as specific bedroom décor for children. My parents would have been astonished at the idea of wallpaper and sheets emblazoned with Disney characters. Instead, we had Toile de Jouy wallpaper (with pastoral themes of the ancient French countryside) in our rooms, which I loved because I'd seen it in my grandparents' house in French Brittany, and it always reminded me of them and made me feel grown up, too. Toile de Jouy patterns are designed to tell a story, and when I'd have trouble falling asleep, I'd look at the walls and it felt like I could always spot a new detail. It was totally enchanting.

Winding Down Before Bedtime

Every person is different, but here are the things that work for me:

- ♥ I turn off my electronic devices at least an hour before bed. The light (and what you're reading) is much too overstimulating. At the end of the day, your brain needs a break!
- ♥ There is nothing better than reading a good book to relax your body and mind to ease you to sleep.
- ♥ There is always a notepad and pencil on my nightstand so I can write anything that I have in mind or to put on my to-do lists. The second I write it down on the pad, it's out of my mind, so I don't have to think about remembering it anymore. This helps me relax.

- ♥ I always have a humidifier going so I know my skin and sinuses will be as hydrated as possible.
- ♥ I keep my bedroom fresh, tidy, and ideally with as few things as possible. I try to follow the advice from Dr. Ana Krieger as well as the feng shui rules that Hélène Weber taught me, which you can read about in this chapter.

Dr. Ana Krieger on Your Basic Sleep Needs

Dr. Ana Krieger, MD, MPH, FCCP, FAASM, is the medical director of the Center for Sleep Medicine at New York-Presbyterian/Weill Cornell Medical Center as well as an associate professor of clinical medicine in the departments of Medicine, Neurology, and Genetic Medicine. In treating sleep disorders, Dr. Krieger believes in a holistic approach, as well as an individualized treatment plan.

Basic Sleep Facts

According to the latest medical research, during adulthood there are actually no major differences in physiological sleep needs until age sixty-five and beyond. The National Sleep Foundation recently released a consensus statement on the recommended sleep duration for the population based on scientific evidence, once again highlighting the fact that actual sleep needs are very individual. Based on this evidence, adults under age sixty-five should avoid sleeping less than six hours or more than ten hours per day. For adults over age sixty-five, the recommended sleep duration is between five and nine hours a day.

Another important consideration is the variability of sleep duration that an individual may be subjected to during their lifetime. Several factors modulate our sleep needs, including physical activity levels, overall health status, and underlying medical or psychiatric problems, among others.

The most common sleep disorder seen in women is insomnia. This is quite prevalent in adult women, more so than in men, as they are often juggling so many different things that they can't stop worrying at night, which impedes their ability to fall asleep. In some cases, underlying sleep disorders, such as restless leg syndrome (particularly common among pregnant women), periodic limb movements in sleep, or sleep apnea are uncovered during these evaluations. Despite being more frequently present in men, some women do develop sleep apnea after menopause. Therefore, we encourage women that have a new onset of snoring after menopause to discuss that with their doctors and determine if a sleep evaluation is needed.

During and pre-menopause, there are hormonal changes that may affect some women more than others. There are also major changes in the body's ability to regulate temperature. Both can result in sleep disturbances.

Awareness is the key for understanding and fixing sleep problems. Women often feel trapped by so many conflicting needs in their lives and start stealing time from sleep, either by effectively scheduling tasks for the nighttime (often after the kids are asleep) or by using the sleep time to think, worry, or plan the days and weeks ahead. This phenomenon is often considered unavoidable by many. However, when taking time to analyze their detailed routine, we often identify opportunities for improving sleep patterns and prevent activities that impair sleep quality at night—for example, by reallocating the time to worry from the bedtime to the daytime. When we sleep better, we perform better, and with improved performance, it is easier to steal a few minutes from our daytime schedule to deal with issues that would otherwise fill our minds at bedtime and keep us from sleeping.

Golden Rules to Improve Your Sleep Regardless of Age

♥ Avoid late or spicy meals.

♥ Avoid exercising too close to bedtime.

♥ Minimize alcohol intake at night, as it leads to sleep fragmentation and sometimes sleep apnea.

♥ Unwind for at least a few minutes, in the dark, before going to bed.

♥ Keep the bedroom temperature below 71 degrees Fahrenheit.

♥ Follow a regular schedule for sleep.

♥ Get up at the same time every day.

♥ Stay active during the day and avoid napping.

A Few Extra Sleep Rules for Children and Teenagers

♥ Lead by example and create a structured household sleep schedule.

♥ Have an open and honest conversation with your children about the need for adequate sleep.

♥ Avoid lengthy bedtime routines—keep them short and sweet.

♥ Do not allow the use of electronics in bed. It's best to stop using them at least an hour before bedtime.

♥ When doing homework or reading on computers or electronics late at night, use glasses to block blue light, or get a blue-light filter for the screens.

♥ Ensure their beds are comfortable for sleep. They should be free of clutter or devices.

Getting Back into a Healthy Routine After a Few Bad Nights

Everyone can have a night where it's hard to fall or stay asleep due to issues at work, stress, or being sick. When that happens:

♥ Stop worrying about sleep, as the more you think about the sleep you're not getting, the harder it will be to fall asleep.

♥ Set up a realistic schedule for sleep.

♥ Avoid snoozing and avoid naps.

♥ Resume exercise and stay active during the day.

Feng Shui Master Hélène Weber on How to Make Your Bedroom More Sleep-Friendly and Toxin-Free

Hélène Weber studied authentic feng shui at the Mastery Academy of Chinese Metaphysics and became a master of feng shui in 2005. (This requires at least seven years of study, much like the study of medicine!) Many of her clients live in London, Paris, and Geneva, and for them, she is their veritable "doctor of the home." These are her most important tips for making your bedroom a haven of rest:

Take the Time Necessary to Arrange Your Bedroom Properly

Though it takes a great deal of effort to set up your bedroom properly, it's worth it since you spend one-third of every day asleep in it. Your bedroom deserves special attention in order for your nights to be as beautiful as your days. Feng shui is not the same as room décor, and a very ugly room can still be very feng shui!

Understanding Yin and Yang

The yang (rising energy: light sources, the sun, the sky, man, heat, mountains, life, summer) and the yin (descending energy: shadow, the moon, the earth, woman, cold, water, death, winter) are in constant opposition.

Find the Best Location for Your Bedroom

♥ First, the bedroom should ideally be located as far as possible from the entryway. In fact, the more you advance into a home, the more the energy of the exterior and entryway (the yang) calms, and the rooms become yin.

♥ We understand, of course, that a bedroom requires a sense of calm. The room must remain the location that is the most yin of all of the rooms in the house. In a house with multiple stories you should select an upstairs room.

♥ Avoid rooms close to loud streets, as an excess of yang will trouble you.

♥ If you have large windows, consider installing shutters or heavy curtains for nighttime. In the summer, protect this room from sunlight and too much yang.

Figure Out the Orientation of Your Bed

♥ Never sleep with your feet facing the door. In China, this is the placement of a coffin! This will cause powerful stagnations in energy. If you are unable to change the orientation of your bed, you can place a screen at the foot of the bed to obstruct this energy flow.

♥ Never sleep with a window or an opening behind your head. You will lose some sense of security and you risk sleeping badly.

♥ In feng shui, the "black turtle" protects our back. This is translated into having a solid wall behind your head to sleep well. An interesting anecdote is that this sense of comfort from a solid wall behind the bed may be a legacy from prehistoric times; the man who rested imprudently with his back to the cavern entrance was the first carried off by nocturnal predators or the first killed by enemy arrows. This fear has remained programmed into our primitive brain functions, which would explain why we feel the need for this sense of protection to sleep soundly. To reinforce this sense of safety, consider installing a headboard.

♥ For the energy to circulate well, consider not having a bed that is too low to the ground (futon style) compared to the rest of the furniture in your room. Try to equalize the heights of the furniture by placing a frame beneath the futon.

♥ All pastel colors—salmon, pale pink, ivory, sea foam, bright blue, and pale yellow—are recommended.

Errors to Avoid in Your Bedroom

♥ Remove the mirrors from your room! In fact, mirrors, or even anything that could reflect your bed (a TV screen or a computer, a lacquered or shiny piece of furniture) renders the environment yang, which can disturb your rest. If you choose very thick curtains for your window, and no light penetrates into the bedroom while you sleep, then it's all right to have shiny furniture; just forget the mirrors.

♥ Red or vibrant colors do not belong in a bedroom, as they are too yang.

♥ No shiny shelving or furniture above the bed, as they can provoke headaches and insomnia.

A Bedroom Must Not Become an Office, a Home Gym, or a Laundry Room

♥ Your bedroom should remain a singular destination: for sleeping or making love.

♥ According to the principles of feng shui, it is important to remove exercise equipment. If you use it, it is better to place it in the bathroom.

♥ Do not use your bedroom as an office, where you or your

significant other make a habit of working all day long. For those who love working in their beds, you can still do this from time to time and bring your work documents to the bedroom, but make sure this remains an occasional activity and that your real office is established elsewhere in the home.

No matter how big or small your bedroom is, at the end of the day the most important thing to remember is that it is a haven for your mind and body to regenerate. What helps me the most in such a large and noisy city as New York is to be able to at least control my bedroom's environment—I remove all the digital devices like my phone and laptop an hour before bed; I keep the room dark at night; and I make sure it is very tidy, with not too many extraneous decorative elements that can be distracting (and need a lot of dusting!). I have also my rituals that help me get into sleep mode. A few long stretches; a lovely scented cream for my body, kept in a jar on my bedside table so I never forget to use it; a good book that helps my brain unwind.

Taking the time to create your own nighttime rituals and doing them will put your entire body in the mood for sleep without fail.

Chapter 10

Our World of Perfume

> *But, when nothing subsists of an old*
> *past, after the death of people, after the*
> *destruction of things, alone, frailer but*
> *more enduring, more immaterial, more*
> *persistent, more faithful, smell and taste*
> *still remain for a long time, like souls,*
> *remembering, waiting, hoping, on the*
> *ruin of all the rest, bearing without giving*
> *way, on their almost impalpable droplet,*
> *the immense edifice of memory.*
>
> —MARCEL PROUST, *SWANN'S WAY*

There is nothing more French than perfume. It is at the heart of what you decide to share with the world as a woman. It can leave you uplifted, exuberant, and refreshed. A sudden whiff can instantly transport you back in time, triggering scent memories that you'd completely forgotten. As Marcel Proust said, perfume is "that last and best reserve of the past, the one which when all our tears have run dry, can make us cry again."

French women, in fact, grow up being taught that what my

mother calls "the timeless power and allure of perfume" is an indispensable part of their essence as a woman. She also refers to a good perfume as being like that perfect little black dress, or the accessory that makes you feel especially beautiful.

> **LORRAINE:** It is invisible, yet its presence is undeniable, luring the gaze with greater power than a beautiful dress or an enticing figure. Heads turn in its wake as it passes. None are immune, none with armor strong enough to withstand the arrow that pierces the heart, like a memory, which seems able to plunge to the end of one's soul . . .
>
> An atmosphere, or a rather a note one wishes to wear, not only to please oneself but also to seduce. This is what perfume is. It bears the signature of one's personality, leaving behind an engraving on the hearts of those you've encountered. More than anything, perfumes open the door to the most sensitive and secret part of the other.

My grandmother understood this concept perfectly, which is why, every Christmas since my sister and I started to wear perfume—and still, to this day—our Christmas gift from her would be a brand-new bottle of perfume. I never thought that it was a different kind of gift, but now I actually realize that it was unique! Perfumes are expensive, and it is true that during our teenage years and even as young ladies, buying a new bottle of perfume made quite a dent in our budgets. I was so grateful that my grandmother always considered scent as an integral part of a woman's elegance and femininity, so of course she wanted her granddaughters to always leave a wafting *sillage* of perfume in their wake.

I still have the names in my head of the fragrances that accompanied my teenage years. A teenage fragrance is something very precious, and the memories that these notes can trigger are priceless, full of tenderness and nostalgia. These names suddenly come back, one by one, each reminding me of a precise moment of my life. For instance, when my mother brought back home Fleur d'Interdit from Givenchy, I took a whiff, and even though it was a perfume created for young girls, it still had a certain naughty sensuality to it, and whenever I smell it now, I can see my much younger self wanting so badly to be grown up. I close my eyes and I am fifteen years old again, when everything— school grades, friendships, boyfriends, drama, and perfume, of course—was so overwhelming in the moment and I thought I would never grow up and push past it all!

The mid-1990s for me will be forever linked to some of these perfumes: Cabotine from Grès with the unusual oval shape of its bottle and lovely green flowers on top, smelling of ginger lily; it was light, easy to wear, and yet tenacious. There was Benetton Tribu, which was like a Mediterranean breeze, and Anaïs Anaïs from Cacharel, with its top notes of orange blossom and hyacinth that made it one of the most popular floral perfumes of my generation. My friends and I had a good giggle over Jean-Paul Gaultier's eponymous scent, which came in a bottle shaped like a woman's body clad in an iconic corset, something we found so sexy and daring!

Summer fragrances such as Elizabeth Arden Sunflowers or Acqua di Gió by Giorgio Armani were appealing, as they had fabulous accords of citrus. My classmates chose others that had such distinctive notes that I could smell them coming and going as they hurried down the hall between classes. There was Thierry Mugler's Angel (with its infamous chocolate top note), L'Eau d'Issey from Issey Miyake (with its ozone note that reminded me of the seaside), or Bvlgari Eau Parfumée au Thé Vert (lovely, fresh, and green, like the tea).

And then, of course, came all the evocative scents worn by the boys we liked in high school and college. I don't remember much about them, but I do remember the vivid woody and floral musk scent of Déclaration by Cartier, as well as the fresh and spicy scent of XS by Paco Rabanne.

After college, my nose became more refined as I started working for beauty companies, where my colleagues were obsessed with fragrance and loved talking about new scent treasures they had uncovered in their travels. When I was at Carolina Herrera, I wore her first perfume, Carolina, and adored its elegant notes of jasmine and tuberose.

Once I moved to Paris, joining the Christian Dior offices, I made a terrible perfume mistake one day. I was still wearing Chanel's Chance, as I found it so uplifting when I spritzed some on every morning on my way to work. One morning I was waiting for the elevator when the marketing director for all of Dior's fragrances walked in. He stood next to me, inhaled deeply, and then asked, "Are you wearing a Chanel fragrance? Is it Chance?" I wanted to drop through the floor—I was so embarrassed to be wearing the competition! So I blushed furiously and apologized, making an excuse that I'd run out of the house for a meeting that morning without thinking. I didn't make that mistake again!

Instead, I switched to men's fragrance Dior Homme, which worked surprisingly well on me, as there was something floral and powdery in it that was incredibly seductive. I realized that one of the reasons why I found Dior Homme so appealing because I was at an age when I was becoming more at ease with my own femininity, but I didn't want to wear any perfume that my mother would have worn. Every time I sprayed on my Dior Homme, I felt confident and sexy, knowing that its unusual allure made me stand out, yet in a subtle and very French way. These days, I have become even more drawn to flowery scents, and I love wearing Tuberose Le Jour by Aerin.

RÉGINE: When I worked at French *Vogue*, we'd always recognize the women at our offices by their perfume. Back then, perfumes used to be composed with quite a lot of musk, which was very expensive but which made these fragrances much more potent and lingering. In the morning, going up the stairs or in the elevator, we knew who had already arrived at the office. The editor-in-chief, Edmonde Charles-Roux, who was naturally elegant and extremely cultivated and from a prestigious family in France, wore Chanel; the fashion editor, Françoise de Langlade, who was the epitome of charming, both easy-going and incredibly professional, wore Guerlain's L'Heure Bleu; and the tall, slim, and fabulously chic Susan Train, then the American correspondent for the magazine, always wore Le Dix of Balenciaga.

LORRAINE: I don't feel that I'm totally dressed unless I have my perfume on. Once or twice in a year I'll realize that I forgot my perfume, and I don't feel at ease. I always have a little fragrance in my bag. If I go somewhere where I don't like the smell, I put some on and instantly feel better. I even use a spritz of it in the car, because we drive a lot more in Paris than in New York, and my car is like the extension of home.

My daughters love this—I have a special closet in my apartment in Paris that is dark and cool, where I keep the remnants of my favorite fragrance that isn't made anymore. Sometimes I go there, and I just inhale it. It's so nice. I still have Vent Vert from Balmain, which was just to die for; it was like a green tonic, so fresh and crisp, and it was something that made you want to get up and go out into the world with confidence. I also have Valentino de Valentino, Gin Fizz from Lubin, some Guerlinades that were given to me by Jean-Paul Guerlain himself.

When I interviewed Maryll Lanvin, from the couture house Lanvin, many years ago, the first thing that struck me when I arrived at her apartment was how wonderful it smelled. I was *subjuguée*—captivated. She had her own perfume burner in the house. For her, and for so many other French women, the art of at-home scents and perfumes are as important as a nicely decorated dinner table and wonderful meal. They're all part of that *art de vivre*.

When I first started working in the business, French perfumes were dominant until the 1970s. Among the French classics, you were always able to find perfumes that changed subtly on each wearer depending on the woman's unique skin chemistry, like a different kind of music.

Then the Americans launched successful fragrances like Charlie by Revlon. These were composed of primarily monolithic notes, which do not vary much from one person to another. By the end of the 1970s, Giorgio of Beverly Hills arrived with a splash on the market. It was unbelievably strong, and so distinctive and unwavering that you could smell it from across a crowded restaurant and know exactly what it was. That was the beginning of the American influence on the perfume industry, and it had a huge effect on the European market. The French had to accept that they were not alone in dominating this market anymore, and the result was the launch of Dior's equally strong and distinctive Poison, as well as the bold fragrance Opium by Yves Saint Laurent.

Many women adored these fragrances back then, and still do today, but I was quite happy to remain loyal to my Valentino or Vent Vert or one of my beloved Guerlain perfumes.

THE TIMELESS POWER AND
ALLURE OF PERFUME

Perfume isn't just about smelling wonderful yourself. For the French, it started off as a very necessary accessory to keep the stench of others at bay. During much of its history, Paris, like all the other big cities of Europe, was notorious for its noxious odors—raw sewage, horse droppings, smoke from countless fires, and, of course, hordes of unwashed bodies. Only the French royals were able to afford custom fragrances, which scented not only their bodies but their apparel and accessories (even their wigs!), as well as furniture and walls, as a new industry was born.

Fortunately, perfumes are easier to buy now. My grandmother loved her Miss Dior, and my mother loved her Valentino, which has a melon top note. They were their signature scents. My sister has one as well—she's been wearing Fidji by Guy Laroche since she was sixteen. Even my brother likes to wear wonderful fragrances. What makes me happy and sad at the same time is how his scent lingers on in our apartment for a few days after one of his visits to New York. Even after he's gone, smelling his fragrance makes me think he's still here!

Perfumes have three layers:

- ♥ Top notes: This is what you smell immediately upon use, and it quickly dissipates. Because top notes are so fleeting, you should never buy a perfume based only on a quick whiff, as it won't indicate what the perfume truly smells like.
- ♥ Middle notes: These last for a few minutes and are meant to prepare your nose for the heart of the perfume, which is the base.

♥ Base notes: This is the strongest part of the perfume, and the longest lasting. If you like florals, for example, look for a perfume with a floral-based bottom, rather than a green or woody one, as that is the accord that will stay with you.

Considering there are literally thousands of perfume choices, how can you narrow them down to find one that might become your signature? Start by identifying the kind of scents you like in particular, choosing from one of these categories, or families:

♥ Floral—based on different flowers, either single or blends, usually sweet. This is by far the most popular category and the heart of feminine fragrances.

♥ Hesperidia—fresh and light notes, not particularly sweet.

♥ Oriental/Amber—earthy and musky. A mixture of warmth and sensuality.

♥ Fruity—fruity compositions, usually playful.

♥ Cyprus—fruity or floral accords.

♥ Citrus—tangy orange, lime, and lemon.

♥ Woody—dry and elegant masculine accords.

♥ Aromatic—citrus and spicy accords, usually with virile, masculine notes.

Of course, don't feel that you need to stick to one fragrance family. Perfume should always make you feel uplifted, and choosing one should always be an enjoyable, sensual experience that makes you feel good.

Two Expert French Noses on Choosing a New Perfume

To help you fine-tune your perfume choices, I spoke to Jacques Polge, the revered nose of Chanel, and the man behind such hits as Coco Mademoiselle, Chance, and Allure. His son, Olivier Polge, took over after he retired to become the new Chanel in-house perfumer, and he is the nose behind Chanel's new perfume Gabrielle (a once-a-decade event!).

When we learn to create a perfume, we use the classifications in the category list to memorize the many scents, such as florals (Chanel No. 5), woody (usually men's fragrances, such as Chanel's Bleu), chypre (which originated with Le Chypre by Coty and was followed by the famous Mitsouko by Guerlain), greens (part of the floral family that became their own subcategory with Vent Vert from Balmain), and Orientals (Emeraude by Coty and Guerlain's famous Shalimar). We also learn about the tenacity of certain notes.

My best advice if you do not know where to start in choosing a perfume is to experiment with brands that have already been around for decades. They were created by the true "noses" of the business. Noses are masters of the olfactory arts, all possessing an exceptional sense of smell and a talent for creating or assessing fragrances and compositions. When you are out shopping, get samples and try the perfume at home, not at the perfume counter of a perfumery or department store. You need an "olfactory silence" to properly assess a fragrance.

And last, remember that the moment you truly smell your perfume is when you spray it on yourself. Afterward, it is the people around you who will perceive the scent, so you need to choose a fragrance that makes you feel good when you put it on.

———

If you're ever in Paris, there is a wonderful little shop on the rue Bachaumont called Nose. Their concept is to help their customers find their signature scent, and it is always a wonderful experience to be guided by a trained nose in the search for the perfect perfume.

Nose's co-founder, Nicolas Cloutier, is a wonderful teacher for both perfume beginners and *savants*. This is what I learned:

Women often think that they know what they like or do not like in terms of scent. Very often, women come in for a perfume diagnostic, and they find out that there is patchouli in their perfume, which makes them say, "Oh no, but I hate patchouli!" when in fact they love patchouli and they had no idea that it is the main component of their favorite perfume. People do not know exactly what they like or think they like, and perfume information sources are often complex or erroneous. It is a very layered and idiosyncratic decision, and a diagnostic is the first step to find out what you really like.

We have more choices today than in the past, in terms of variety. To choose a new perfume, you need to understand which of the seven olfactory families works best for you. Usually between the ages of fifteen to twenty-five, women go for the floral/fruity range. After that, between the ages of twenty-five to forty-five, there is the musky, more animal range, which is heavier. After the age of forty-five, women tend to go back to floral notes. (I've found it's the same with makeup; as women age they tend to go lighter.)

To help with your decision, try to learn a few basics. When you put perfume on a test strip or your wrist, first you smell the top notes, which are the green notes, the spicy notes. Then two or three minutes later, you smell the middle notes, which are mostly floral, and five, ten, or even fifteen minutes later, you smell the base notes. Perfumery is chemistry. The size of the molecules matters more than anything, and base notes take a longer time to evaporate because their size is larger, so they weigh more. This is why it can take up to fifteen minutes to fully develop.

You need to take your time to smell properly. I encourage people to smell the different fragrances—take the test strip and leave it on their desk, for example; give it time. Often, the greatest perfumers compose a mix of top/middle/base notes, which becomes their signature scent. You need to let it sit for a while and come back to it the next day. Letting the scent breathe is essential. Sometimes, however, you are going to smell a perfume and you'll have a spontaneous response; you'll just know. Keep an open mind and you might surprise yourself.

After I spoke to Nicolas, I left his shop and wandered around—what we call *flâner* in French, occasionally sniffing one of my wrists because they smelled so good. When I met up later with my mother and grandmother, we happily chatted about the perfumes they loved and all the perfumes we still have yet to try—a topic that will always keep us enthralled for many hours.

Epilogue

What inspires us to do it all? Is it the admiring glances of others? The look of that one special person? Or for ourselves?

It is natural to be affected by those appraising looks bestowed upon us by the people we meet, but we also care about our beauty for ourselves, to make us feel good.

In France, women are lucky, as they often get a sense of appreciation from men. French men love women. French men also love to gaze at women, not in a macho or sexist way but with deep admiration. French women do not make all these efforts just for themselves, because deep down inside they do admit that it gives them great pleasure to know a man will notice their perfume, or lipstick, elegant skirt, or fashionable heels. Male friends can compliment a woman without it being considered out of place. And it is so great for our self-confidence!

Let's remember that often what men like in us are things that we might perceive as weaknesses. Sometimes ultra-perfection can actually scare them. The way a man gazes in admiration at a woman is quite different from how a woman sees herself—or the way women look at each other, which can often be far harsher than men.

Read these lines from Cyril Chapuy, Deputy General Manager L'Oréal Luxe Worldwide, about women and you will understand the essence of the French attitude about them: "My world would be nothing without you. From my very first days, you comforted me and now continue to be my source of inspiration every day, revealing the different sides of who you are: confident, conquering, uncertain, seductive, sensitive, intelligent, and generous. Daily life would be dreary and dull without your sparkle, without your vulnerability and beauty. Your beauty has grown into my passion."

I also believe that some imperfections can be charming, and trying to change your natural look too much never really works. It becomes a bit too stiff because you know, deep down, that it's not really *you*. Being confident in yourself has an allure and softness that will always be attractive.

French women are not afraid to show their true selves; they won't play at being someone other than who they are. They are not afraid to show their individuality; they play with what nature gave them and make the most of it, turning a difference into an asset that may even get better with age! Do it for yourself as much as for others, and you'll reach a stage of equanimity with your appearance. It is about finding that balance that makes us happy in life. We have to learn to treat ourselves kindly.

As my mother recently told me, "As French women, we are perhaps more accepting about growing old, because aging intelligently means accepting one's weaknesses and carrying on nonetheless. Keeping up with the pace of those around you is an act of discipline and helps above all to promote a positive image of the passage of time to younger generations.

"Beauty, when viewed from this angle—with all that it encompasses in terms of care and artifice—isn't the least bit superficial. It is a necessity."

We hope this book helps lift up every woman who reads it, with the advice and tools to make the small changes in their routine that will make them feel beautiful every day.

Régine, Lorraine, and Clémence

Appendix

Resources / Where to Buy Online
Johnlewis.com
Selfridges.com
Harrods.com
Spacenk.co.uk
Libertylondon.com
Netaporter.co.uk
Houseoffraser.co.uk
Debenhams.com
Amazon.co.uk
Boots.co.uk
Superdrug.com

French Beauty Brands
You can buy all these brands online.
Avene.co.uk
Laroche-posay.co.uk
Loreal-paris.co.uk
Joelle-ciocco.com/en
Ingridmillet.com
Leonorgreyl.com/en/GB/page/home
https://christophe-robin.com/en

david-mallett.com/en
kurebazaar.com
bastiengonzalez.com
carita.com

Acknowledgments

This is the best part of the book, where I get to thank all the people around me!

Thank you to all the women in my family whom I love.

Special thanks to my sister, Raphaëlle, as this book began thanks to you!

Thank you to my grandmother and mother, who have always inspired me, and, of course, my daughter for providing the motivation to pursue this book—she is now the recipient of eighty years of beauty advice from her family.

My husband, William. Thank you for all the support and encouragement about everything in life.

My father and brother, who are constant inspirations.

Thank you to my wonderful agent, Rachel, who was there at every step of the way.

My publisher, Zennor, and the brilliant team at Michael Joseph.

My writing partner, Karen Moline.

My girlfriends who inspired me from Paris, London, Geneva, New York, Miami, and San Francisco as well as my friend Béatrice, who shares the office with me and has helped me so much along the way.

The translators and copy editors who were part of it all! Thank you, Françoise Hartman; you have been an incredible source of support for both the magazine and the book. Thank you to Paloma Parkes for your time in between exams.

Thank you to Daniel Wasserman from Word Geek Translation for the translations of some of the key passages of the book as well as the major edits. Thank you to Lisa Dupont who also joined the editing team. You really helped me see the light at the end of the tunnel!

Merci to more family members who helped immensely during this project. Ted and Dini for their expert advice from the title to the book launch. Yannick and Chloé for opening the doors of your home for the three-generations photo shoot.

For the three-generations photograph, thank you to Pamela Berkovic, photographer. Jean-Luc Capon, hairdresser, and Julien Charlier for applying Clémence's hair and makeup. Christine and Bastien at Carita Montaigne for Lorraine and Régine's hair and makeup.

Thank you to all the experts who so generously offered their time, and contributed to making this book a wonderful source of beauty advice for all women: Jacques Polge, Terry de Gunzburg, Dr. Serge Hautier, Dr. Georges Mouton, MD, (gmouton. com), Nicolas Cloutier, Amélie de Bourbon Parme, Nicole Desnoë, Isabelle Bellis (isabellebellis.com), Joëlle Ciocco, Christine from Carita, Muriel Baurens, Elisabeth Bouhadana (a huge *merci*!), Odile Mohen, Dominique Moyal, Bruno Bernard, David Mallett, Christophe Robin, Béatrice Rochelle, Sylvie Ferrari, Colette Pingault, Christophe Marchesseau (excellencedessens. com), Claire Bausset, Béatrice Arapoglou (alias BA), Dr. Hagop Alajajian, DC, Martine de Richeville (martinedericheville.com), Olivier Échaudemaison, Dr. Philippe Allouche (biologique-recherche.com), Dr. Ana C. Krieger, Philippe Simonin (nutriscienceclinic.com), Delphine Prudhomme (institut-francoise-morice.fr), Caroline Meyrignac (orthopedie-meyrignac.fr), Bastien Gonzalez (bastiengonzalez.com), Fatima Zegrani, Hélène Weber, the team from Avène, Dr. Barbara Guedj, Prisca Courtin-Clarins, Frédéric Fekkai, Dr. Jean-Pierre Titon, Daniela Beccaria-Blamey (anamaya.co.uk), Marie-Françoise Stouls (24sevres.com), Dr. Catherine Brémont-Weill and Dr. Sophie Laglenne, Carmel O'Neill (therenewspa.com), Romain Gaillard, co-founder of The Detox Market (thedetoxmarket.com), and the French Institute Alliance Française with Marie-Monique Steckel and her team, who always supported my work.

For the photographs of Régine, Lorraine, and Isabelle Adjani, thank you to the Irving Penn Foundation, the Guy Bourdin family, Jean-Daniel Lorieux, the group Estée Lauder, the Courtin-Clarins family, and the communication team from Christian Dior. Prune Cirelli for the illustrations.

And *bien sur*, thank you to all the experts who I love to see in New York: Shu Rousseau, Salih at Salih Salon, the team from Julien Farrel Salon, Carmel O'Neill at the Renew Spa, Sabrina, Isabelle Bellis, the team from Erika Bloom Studio, Katherine Greiner, Daphné at l'Appartement Caudalie Spa, and Aida Bicaj.

Bibliography

Bailly, Sylvie. *Des siècles de beauté—Entre séduction et politique.* Paris: Editions Jourdan, 2014.

Bona, Dominique. *Colette et les siennes.* Paris: Éditions Grasset, 2017.

Bonilla, Laure-Emmanuelle. *100 ans de coiffure.* France: Éditions Prat, 2009.

Chahine Nathalie, Catherine Jazdzewski, Marie-Pierre Lannelongue, Françoise Mohrt, Fabienne Rousso, and Francine Vormese. *Beauté du siècle.* Paris: Éditions Assouline, 2000.

Fitoussi, Michèle. *Helena Rubinstein: La femme qui inventa la beauté.* Paris: Éditions Grasset, 2010.